Maintaining Strategic Relevance

Career and Technical Education Program Discontinuance in Community and Technical Colleges

Kevin J. Fleming

University Press of America,® Inc.
Lanham • Boulder • New York • Toronto • Plymouth, UK

Copyright © 2015 by University Press of America,® Inc.
4501 Forbes Boulevard, Suite 200, Lanham, Maryland 20706
UPA Acquisitions Department (301) 459-3366

Unit A, Whitacre Mews, 26-34 Stannary Street,
London SE11 4AB, United Kingdom

Library of Congress Control Number: 2014957895
ISBN: 978-0-7618-6530-8 (pbk : alk. paper)—ISBN: 978-0-7618-6531-5 (electronic)

∞™ The paper used in this publication meets the minimum requirements of American
National Standard for Information Sciences Permanence of Paper for Printed Library
Materials, ANSI/NISO Z39.48-1992.

Contents

Preface

The community and technical college and mission requires offering relevant Career & Technical Education (CTE) programs. Due to program accretion and bureaucratic inertia, program discontinuance (PD) seems at odds with postsecondary culture. Yet, as a result of recent budget constrictions, community colleges are forced to identify effective PD processes. This book helps explain under what conditions CTE program discontinuance occurs, including how people felt about the process and the impact of institutional culture. As a proxy for other states, a statewide policy analysis identifies the key elements within existing California Community College PD board policies. Together, the interviews and policy analysis provide context and best practices for practitioners and faculty nationally looking to effectively and appropriately discontinue CTE programs. (Note that the terms community college, technical college, technical institute, and 2-year vocational colleges are considered synonymous for this inquiry, and thus for the ease of consistency the term "community college" is used throughout this text).

Since the California Community College systems provides education to over 1.5 million Americans yearly, and is the largest higher educational system in the world, California was chosen as the location of my research and thus is the central focus of this text. In working with academic professionals in other states, most of the concepts and recommendations herein have been validated to transcend across state lines.

There are two main reasons why I have chosen to write on the characteristics of PD processes and policies in community colleges. The first reason is that except for state education code and one white paper in 1998 (later revised in 2012), there is very little research on community college program discontinuance in my home state of California. The second reason I am passionate about this topic is that as a result of the recession and state budget crisis, now is the first time in three generations that faculty and administrators in the California Community College system (CCC) are forced to rely on effective program discontinuance processes to strategically and appropriately reduce CTE curriculum from their offerings. I selected this topic because my understanding from personal experience and in reading the literature is that many community colleges either rarely discontinue CTE programs, do so without strategic intentionality, and/or their discontinuation process is not following any process/policy. My research taught me the conditions within which community colleges have undergone program discontinuation, what the role of policy was in their process, and how the faculty and administrators involved felt about the PD process. My hope is that the recommendations herein will help other community and technical colleges in establishing and/ or engaging PD processes which strategically and effectively discontinue CTE programs while at the same time making optimal use of the resources (fiscal and human) available to the institution.

The theoretical framework for this book includes Birnbaum's bureaucratic system,[1] and Bolman and Deal's[2] four frames to analyze organizational change. To inform my recommendations, thirty-four interviews were completed from three California community colleges, and 60 district policies throughout the state (83.33%) were cataloged and analyzed to identify the PD process catalysts, appropriate communications, feelings and perceptions, appropriate process durations, and the role of board policy. This research revealed that CTE program discontinuance most commonly occurs: 1) when fiscal resources are reduced externally, 2) when a key administrative catalyst triggers a PD process, 3) when there is no full-time faculty to champion and provide leadership, and/or 4) when the college has a comprehensive annual program review cycle that measures program vitality. Current PD practices seemingly take better care of affected students than the part-time faculty members teaching in the terminated program. Moreover, communication and role clarity are validated to be of paramount importance.

If you are interested in career and technical education, program termination, appropriate strategies to manage the constant churning of CTE programs, college governance, academic discontinuance policies, and/or factors that affect morale during academic program changes, then you have found the correct resource.

NOTES

1. Birnbaum, R. (1989). *How Colleges Work: The Cybernetics of Academic Organization and Leadership*. San Francisco, CA: Jossey-Bass Publishers. And: Birnbaum (2004). "The End of Shared Governance: Looking Ahead or Looking Back." In Tierney W., Lechuga, V. (Fall. 2004). *Restructuring Shared Governance in Higher Education*, New Directions in Higher Education, #127, Jossey Bass. P. 5–22.

2. Bolman, L. & Deal, T. (1997). *Reframing Organizations*. San Francisco: Jossey-Bass. and: Bolman, L. & Deal, T. (2008). *Reframing Organizations:* Artistry, Choice and Leadership. San Francisco: Jossey-Bass.

Acknowledgments

To my mother, who shaped me into the man I am today.

To my wife, whose unwavering support and love made this possible.

To my colleagues and peers for your guidance and participation.

To the giants upon whose shoulders I stand.

All glory to God through whom all things are possible.

Introduction

The community colleges have a vital mission to provide postsecondary education to the vast majority of Californians. The Master Plan for Higher Education in California 1960–1975 differentiated the three-tiered system of postsecondary education: The University of California system, the California State University system, and the California Community College system. The plan established the primary missions for the state's community colleges to provide open access, lower-division pre-baccalaureate, and career & technical education. California Education code, Section 66010.4(a)(1) presently maintains that the two primary missions of 2-year community colleges are transfer preparation and career & technical education (CTE).

The fulfillment of half of this mission requires community colleges to offer CTE programs that are both effective and relevant to their regional economy. Providing effective workforce educational programs require colleges to constantly revise, create, and delete CTE certificates and degree options. While the general education curriculum typically does not significantly change from year to year, technical programs such as healthcare and computer technology require diligent efforts to keep up with the changes and advances occurring in industry.

THE PROBLEM

Since the California Community College (CCC) system has been largely in growth-mode since the end of World War II, an accretion of academic programs has occurred. Not surprisingly, the CCC system has sufficient processes and protocols for creating and modifying CTE programs (as required by California Education Code §55130 and §78016). The California Community College Chancellor's Office maintains an updated database of existing aca-

1

demic programs across all 112 colleges noting their year of creation. However, the system does not have parallel processes or protocols to discontinue CTE programs. In fact, program discontinuance seemingly goes against the bureaucratic inertia firmly rooted in the community college culture. Yet some programs are in fact discontinued; presumably as a result of external pressures and a reduction in available funding. But without a unified policy and effective program vitality review processes, CTE programs may be discontinued for the wrong reasons. As the old adage cautions, programs may be cut with an ax instead of a scalpel. Just how do community colleges go about the business of deciding which programs are the least precious?

Not since the 1940s have community colleges been forced to reduce course and program offerings the way the constrained state budget is requiring colleges to do today. Thus, interest in program discontinuance (PD) processes and policies have recently increased in order to provide community colleges with the proper guidance/support in contracting all academic curriculum offerings, including CTE programs. This research aims to learn how and why PD occurs so that community colleges can learn to do so while maintaining the strategic relevance of their CTE offerings.

Moreover, some researchers in the field propose that community colleges provide an overabundance of curricular options which causes students to be overwhelmed by the complexity of the system,[1] thus ultimately delaying or thwarting their progress toward program completion.[2] For example, Harvard University offers bachelor's degree programs in only 43 academic fields (and requires all students to complete a core curriculum), while nearby Bunker Hill Community College offers 72 programs with no commonly required core and many offerings available on-line.[3] In California, Riverside Community College District in Southern California offers 190 different certificate and degree programs; few of which align to other 2-year or 4-year institutions.

As Rosenbaum, Deil-Amen, and Person observe, "Although community colleges offer many choices, we find that they rarely offer one: highly structured programs that curtail choice but promise timely graduation and an appropriate job."[4] More often than not students often gain information by taking courses almost at random, do not receive enough information about prerequisites or program requirements, and over 25% of students are unsure which courses count towards specific degree requirements.[5] Moreover, the unstructured complexity found in many community college catalogs results in an unintentional information barrier which is most likely very daunting for disadvantaged populations requiring remediation (whom these institutions primarily serve).

DEFINITION OF TERMS

California Community College Chancellor's Office (CCCCO): The California Community College Chancellor's Office is the coordinating office for the California community college system granted governance authority through California Education Code. Also referred to as the "State Chancellor's Office."

Career & Technical Education (CTE): Academic programs that prepare students for gainful employment within a specific occupation are called Career & Technical Education. Career & Technical Education courses/programs are differentiated from general education courses/programs by the California Community College Chancellor's Office (CCCCO) using unique identification codes.

Community College (or College): There are currently 112 community colleges in California. Community colleges are 2-year public institutions organized within independent "single-college districts" or "multi-college districts." Academic programs are offered by a given college, not by its district.

Community College Districts (or District): The 112 California community colleges are organized within 72 districts, each with their own locally elected Boards of Trustees. Some districts are comprised of just one community college. Community college board policies and administrative procedures are adopted per district, not per college.

Program: California Title 5 section §55000(g) defines an educational program as "an organized sequence of courses leading to a defined objective, a degree, a certificate, a diploma, a license, or transfer to another institution of higher learning." The unit of analysis in this research is an approved CTE academic program which could be a locally-approved certificate (under 18 units), a state-approved certificate (12 units or more), and/or an Associate's Degree (60 units). Individual courses, categorical initiatives, contract education trainings, or student affairs programs (such as EOPS or T3P), are excluded from this research's definition.

Program Discontinuance (PD or discontinuance): The deletion of an academic program by a specific district's Board of Trustees resulting in it being removed from college catalogs, publications, and no longer being able to award the certificate/degree to students is called program discontinuance.

Program Discontinuance Policy: A program discontinuance policy is a governance policy approved by the district's Board of Trustees and publically available on their district website providing guidance/procedures for reviewing and deleting academic programs. Occasionally referred to as, "Program Vitality and Discontinuance" policies.

NOTES

1. Scott-Clayton, J. (January, 2011). *The Shapeless River: Does a Lack of Structure Inhibit Student's Progress at Community Colleges?* Community College Research Center, Paper No. 25. Teachers College, Columbia University.

2. Tinto, V. (1993). *Leaving College: Rethinking the causes and cures of student attrition (2nd Ed.).* Chicago, IL: University of Chicago Press.

3. Rosenbaum, J., Deil-Amen, R., and Person, A. (2006). *After Admission: From college access to college success.* New York, NY: Russell Sage Foundation.

4. Rosenbaum, J., Deil-Amen, R., and Person, A. (2006). *After Admission: From college access to college success.* New York, NY: Russell Sage Foundation, p. 21.

5. Ibid.

Chapter One

The Evolving Role of CTE

In order to understand effective program discontinuance processes of CTE programs, it is first pivotal to understand the unique history and current role these program have within American higher education.

The phrase "vocational education" has slowly been replaced by "career education" and again more recently by "career & technical education." By definition, CTE describes courses and programs designed to prepare students for employment opportunities that do not initially require a 4-year degree. Several outdated assumptions cloud the present understanding of CTE's role. Firstly, too many people seem to think of CTE programs as being limited to working with one's hands and requiring less intellectual effort. Others have a fallacious image of CTE being nothing but studying one's hobby (e.g. woodworking). These misconceptions stem from the 1950s-70s when vocational education concentrated mostly on teaching about job-specific tools and techniques in preparation for a specific job in the workplace.[1] During this time, tools and techniques did not change very much and industry was pleased with productive workers graduating from these programs. Fortunately, the hands-on approach encouraged many to stay in school and complete a college certificate/degree. Unfortunately many of these technically focused students left without a clear understanding of the fundamentals of math, English, and science. With few exceptions, these programs taught the *how* (tactile skills) without the *why* (abstract theories). According to Hull and Parnell, when their positions later evolved, many then found themselves in the 1980's lacking the skills needed in the beginnings of a fast-changing technological society.[2]

As a result of this historical "tactile skill" focus, a majority of researchers, including well-intentioned educators and practitioners, still perceive a false dichotomy within the American educational system; namely vocational education being for the "dumb kids" and so-called academic education for the "smart" ones.[3] This subconscious perception of dumb/smart classes impacts the required curriculum as well. About twice as many jobs require welding as a background skill for employment than jobs which require background skills in chemistry, yet nearly every school invests in expensive chemistry labs and requires chemistry courses even though the content has less than half the potential as welding in contextualizing science principles while providing an occupational skill.[4] Why is this so? Some educational leaders assert it is in large part due to the preconceived notions and bias towards the Platonic versus Aristotelian approach of general education. Alfred North Whitehead asked, "if education is not useful, what is it?" The answer, of course, is that all students are ultimately preparing themselves for a vocation as a surgeon, carpenter, secretary, teacher, nurse, tax preparer, etc. To suggest that general knowledge for its own sake is somehow superior to useful or applied knowledge is simply absurd.

High school CTE instructors routinely complain that many counselors perceive "shop" courses as the dumping ground for those with behavioral problems or poor motivation. In truth, many of the behavioral and motivational problems initially occur because students, "see little purpose, slight meaning, and meager real-world application" in their secondary academic courses.[5] With the widespread promulgation of the 'every child will go to college' mentality (also known as the 'one way to win' paradigm), many children within the neglected majority feel marginalized and end up dropping out of school.[6] If there ever was a time when we could be satisfied preparing some students for work and others for higher learning, then that time has passed. With recent dialog focusing on student success, "disrupting the false dichotomy between career preparation and college preparation can [help to] disrupt enduring inequities."[7]

Almost thirty years ago, America's collective conscious was awakened in 1983 with the popular publication, *A Nation At Risk*, which is cited as helping to define the problems afflicting American education including the diluted, purposeless "general track" education.

> Secondary school curricula have been homogenized, diluted, and diffused to the point that they no longer have a central purpose. In effect, we have a cafeteria style curriculum in which the appetizers and desserts can easily be mistaken for the main courses. Students have migrated from vocational and college preparatory programs to "general track" courses in large numbers. The proportion of students taking a general program of study has increased from 12 percent in 1964 to 42 percent in 1979.[8]

Shortly after its publication, commissions were then formed, research studies conducted, and ambitious programs were undertaken to reform K-12 and community college education.[9] The structure of vocational education was completely rethought in the 1980s and 1990s resulting in applied-academic courses which infused relevant hands-on instruction with academically rigorous science, communications, and math. Thus, Career & Technical Education was born. The 'concrete' learner is still heavily engaged in learning valuable skills along with mastering the associated, relevant principals. For over 20 years, CTE has taken root from grant-funded projects, pilot sites, charter schools, and exemplary institutions.[10] Academic subject matter became presented in the context of how it is utilized in personal and work-based situations. For the first time, it became both possible and practical for students to experience a career-oriented educational curriculum that provided them with the foundational tools and techniques of a particular field along with the academic acumen to continue their studies towards a two or four-year degree. Hull and Parnell say it best in their statement,

> No longer can we speak of the liberal arts versus the practical arts as though we live and learn in separate worlds. The students of the future will require both. If we fail to match in any systematic way the goals of schooling with the real-life needs of individuals living in a knowledge-rich but application-poor society, we will fail in our educational calling. All our young people of today require first-rate educational programs that prepare them for that next step after high school-whether that step is a job, an associate-degree program in a community college, or a baccalaureate degree in a university.[11]

I believe that a balance of both CTE and liberal arts is needed at every educational level. Students enrolled in technical programs need academic rigor, just as honors students need abstract information contextualized in real-life applications. It is no longer appropriate or acceptable to train a citizen for a specific occupation while lacking the associated academic foundation as burgeoning technological demands will certainly pass them by. Similarly, it is equally unacceptable (or at least it should be) to educate a citizen with abstract academic knowledge absent any career proficiencies or earning-potential competencies. It is no longer an either/or proposition; all students need both, and the separation of the two has been to the advantage of neither.

Thus the primary purpose of Career & Technical Education as documented in research publications is in actuality to help connect information and knowledge with real-life experiences and to prepare students to be productive members of the American workforce. "Connectedness, context, and continuity are key words in reshaping curricula and improving the education program, particularly for the two middle quartiles of students."[12] But how does a community college identify the right mix of programs to offer which best serve their local communities?

NEEDED: A HIGHLY SKILLED WORK FORCE

Over the past two decades, many of the low-skilled manual labor jobs in America have either been outsourced or automated. To remain competitive globally, there is little debate that America needs more college graduates in the future.[13] Yet, some caution that this projected need should not be automatically assumed to mean more citizens need to achieve a bachelor's degree education or higher. Nationally, total employment is expected to increase by 10 percent from 2008 to 2018. However, these 15.3 million jobs expected to be added by 2018 will not be evenly distributed across major industry groups or required levels of educational obtainment.[14]

According to Harvard's recent study, *Pathways to Prosperity*, only 33% of all jobs in the future will require a Bachelor's degree or higher, while the overwhelming majority (77%) will require technical skills and training at the Associates Degree level, or below.[15] Other statistics that account for the number of Americans who hold a BA or higher (approximately 32%) are deceiving as they do not account for the many college-educated people who are underemployed. While over 60% of Americans in existing jobs have obtained 'some college' or a postsecondary credential/degree (The College Board, 2010), only 36% of all jobs *require* a Bachelors degree, or more.[16]

Recent research identifies that the majority of positions that pay middle-class wages require skills associated with at least some education beyond high school.[17] Many of these high-skilled, family-supporting occupations in California are called "middle-skilled jobs," requiring more than a high school education but less than a four-year degree. Some reports show that middle-skill jobs represent the largest share of jobs in California - some 49 percent - and the largest share of future job openings. However there is growing evidence of a *skills gap* in which many young Americans are not receiving the hands-on training and work ethics they need.[18] Some have calculated that, "the percentage of teens and young adults who have jobs is now at the lowest level since World War II."[19] High skilled entry-level and technician jobs today require individuals that have a wide range of knowledge, technical skills, and problem solving ability that the average high school education simply does not provide.

According to the Department of Labor, of the thirty fastest growing occupations between 2008-2018, all will require some education beyond high school (such as home health aides, biomedical engineers, dental hygienists, pharmacy technicians, and environmental engineer technicians).[20] But only 14 of the 30 will require education at, or beyond, a 4-year baccalaureate degree. The other sixteen of the fastest growing 30 jobs in America will require CTE education via either a postsecondary vocational certificate or an Associate's Degree. In fact, according to recent national publications, over half of the fastest growing occupations in America do not require a Bachelors degree.

Occupational growth can be considered in two ways: by the rate of growth (fastest growing) and/or by the number of new jobs created. Some jobs may have both a fast growth rate and create a large number of new jobs. But, many occupations which employ few workers might experience a fast percentage of growth although the resulting numerical growth of new jobs may be insignificant. So, community colleges should look at the occupations with the largest numerical growth. According to the Bureau of Labor Statistics in projecting the 2008-18 period, the "most" jobs are significantly different than those of the "fastest growing."[21] Only five of the top twenty require education at or above a Bachelors degree. The remaining fifteen require career & technical education in the form of certificates, Associate Degrees, or on-the-job training.

Amongst every educational category, occupations in the associate degree category are projected to grow the fastest, at about 19 percent between 2008-18. This is a greater percentage growth than Masters degrees, Bachelor's degrees, or professional degrees. The actual needs of America's industries are not in alignment with the "every student needs a Bachelor's degree" rhetoric found in many recent publications.[22] Simply sending more students to college will not change the types of jobs required by our economy, and the college-for-all ideology cannot change the reality of the occupational distributions in the labor market.

For generations, some research publications and conventional wisdom has resulted in parents encouraging their children to go to college, any college, to major in anything, under the assumption the investment would yield economic success. But with rising education costs, a shrinking job market, and oversaturation of some majors in the workforce, many have begun to question if we have more college graduates than we need. Articles such as the New York Times' May, 2010 piece "Plan B: Skip College," The Washington Post's September, 2010 story, "Some say bypassing higher education is smarter than paying for a degree," The Chronicle of Higher Education's October 2010 story, "Here's Your Diploma. Now Here's Your Mop," and even viral videos from Mike Rowe, the host of 'Dirty Jobs' promoting CTE education (mikeroweworks.com), the 2013 animated video "Success in the New Economy" posted on vimeo.com, and Sir Ken Robinson advocating for the reform of education (ted.com), all raise this question in different ways. Educators overwhelmingly agree that America does need to increase those continuing beyond high school, but often times the transition from the research to common vernacular results in combining all levels of postsecondary achievement together into a "university for all" sentiment. In segmenting out each level of postsecondary achievement (some college, certificate, Associates, Bachelors, Masters, Professional degree), we see that the largest percentage of our workforce needs a CTE certificate or Associate's degree, not a 4-year Bachelor's degree.

This projected need in highly-skilled employees at the career & technical education level is juxtaposed with employers clamoring for additionally skilled workers. A recent study funded by the Lumina Foundation and the Bill and Melinda Gates Foundation interviewed human resources directors and senior executives to determine the basic knowledge and applied skills needed for new entrants into the 21st century workforce in America. Less than a quarter of employers—only 23.9 percent—reported that new entrants with four-year college degrees have "excellent" basic knowledge and applied skills, citing numerous important deficiencies. Perhaps surprisingly, the study's findings indicated that applied skills such as information technology application, innovation, and problem solving at all educational levels, "trump basic knowledge and skills such as reading comprehension and mathematics."[23] To many employers, one's diploma often serves as little more than a certificate of attendance.[24] This further illustrates that America is experiencing a skills-gap between what our educational system provides students and what employers expect in order for individual workers to be successful.

While the purpose of education is certainly not solely to satisfy the changing needs of industry, the critical workforce issues and dire skills-gap in today's marketplace should not be ignored. In fact, some claim the needs of industry and the demands of postsecondary education have converged and it is misaligned state policy that is stalling progress.[25] Educators at all levels need to be reminded that the majority of the population will never earn a baccalaureate degree nor do they need one in order to secure middle-class wages.[26] Those students that do not initially earn a 4-year degree still want, and deserve, an excellent education—but one that is applicable to their individual talents and abilities in alignment with opportunities in the labor market.

NOTES

1. Hull, D. & Parnell, D. (1991). *Tech Prep Associate Degree: A Win/Win Experience.* Texas: The Center for Occupational Research and Development.

2. Ibid.

3. Deil-Amen, R. & DeLuca, S. (2010). "The Underserved Third: How Our Educational Structures Populate an Educational Underclass." *Journal of Education for Students Placed at Risk*, 15: 27–50. And: Rose. M. (2008). Blending "hand work" and "brain work": Can multiple pathways deepen learning? In J. Oakes & M. Saunders (Eds.), *Beyond tracking: Multiple pathways to college, career, and civic participation* (pp. 21–35). Cambridge, MA: Harvard Education Press.

4. Parnell, D. (1985). *The Neglected Majority*. Washington D.C.: The Community College Press.

5. Hull, D. & Parnell, D. (1991). *Tech Prep Associate Degree: A Win/Win Experience.* Texas: The Center for Occupational Research and Development, p. 5.

6. Gray, K. & Herr, E. (2006). *Other Ways to Win: Creating Alternatives for High School Graduates. Third Edition.* Thousand Oaks: Corwin Press.

7. Deil-Amen, R. & DeLuca, S. (2010). "The Underserved Third: How Our Educational Structures Populate an Educational Underclass." *Journal of Education for Students Placed at Risk*, 15: 27–50.

8. NCEE (1983). *A Nation At Risk: The Imperative for Education Reform.* A Report to the Nation and the Secretary of Education by The National Commission on Excellence in Education, p. 21.

9. Hull, D. & Parnell, D. (1991). *Tech Prep Associate Degree: A Win/Win Experience.* Texas: The Center for Occupational Research and Development.

10. Scott, J., and Sarkees-Wircenski, M. (2004). *Overview of Career and Technical Education: Third Edition.* Homewood, Illinois: American Technical Publishers, Inc.

11. Hull, D. & Parnell, D. (1991). *Tech Prep Associate Degree: A Win/Win Experience.* Texas: The Center for Occupational Research and Development, p. 9.

12. Ibid, p. 15.

13. Carnevale, A. & Rose, S. (2011). *The Undereducated American.* Washington D.C.: Georgetown University's Center on education and the Workforce. And: Carnevale, A., & Smith, N. (2011). *Career Clusters: Forecasting Demand for High School Through College Jobs 2008-2018.* Washington D.C.: Georgetown University's Center on Education and the Workforce.

14. Bureau of Labor Statistics (2010). *Occupational Outlook Handbook 2010-11 Edition.* U.S. Department of Labor.

15. Symonds, W., Schwartz, R., & Ferguson, R. (February 2011). *Pathways to Prosperity: Meeting the Challenge of Preparing Young Americans for the 21st Century.* Report issued by the Pathways to Prosperity Project, Harvard Graduate School of Education.

16. Ibid.

17. Carnevale, A., & Derochers, D. (2003). *Standards for what? The economic roots of K-16 reform.* Princeton, NJ: Educational Testing Service.

18. Symonds, W., Schwartz, R., & Ferguson, R. (February 2011). *Pathways to Prosperity: Meeting the Challenge of Preparing Young Americans for the 21st Century.* Report issued by the Pathways to Prosperity Project, Harvard Graduate School of Education.

19. Ibid, p. 1.

20. Department of Labor (December 8, 2010), *Table 1.3 Fastest Growing Occupations, 2008 and projected 2018.* Employment Projections Program, U.S. Bureau of Labor Statistics. Accessed 7/23/2014 at http://www.bls.gov/emp/ep_table_103.htm.

21. Bureau of Labor Statistics (2010). *Occupational Outlook Handbook 2010-11 Edition.* U.S. Department of Labor.

22. Carnevale, A., & Smith, N. (2011). *Career Clusters: Forecasting Demand for High School Through College Jobs 2008-2018.* Washington D.C.: Georgetown University's Center on Education and the Workforce.

23. The Conference Board. (2006). *Are they Really ready to Work?: Employers' Perspectives on the Basic Knowledge and Applied Skills of New Entrants to the 21st Century U.S. Workforce,* p. 9.

24. Achieve, Inc. (2004). *Ready or Not: Creating a High School Diploma That Counts.* The American Diploma Project.

25. Shulock, N., & Offenstein, J. (2012). *Career Opportunities: Career Technical Education and the College Completion Agenda.* Sacramento, CA: Institute for Higher Education Leadership & Policy.

26. Bosworth, B. (2010). *Certificates Count: An Analysis of Sub-baccalaureate Certificates.* Washington, DC: Complete College America.

Chapter Two

Variables Affecting
CTE Program Offerings

There are a number of variables that affect the mix of CTE program offerings at a given community college. These factors affect the creation, modification, maintenance, and discontinuance of all CTE programs.

INSTRUCTIONAL EQUIPMENT COSTS

Under various titles, beginning in 1917 with the Smith-Hughes Act and later in 1963 as the Vocational Education Act, federal legislation has focused on preparing citizens to develop the skills needed by business and industry. "System leaders, campus heads, faculty and staff, and state lawmakers will all need to engage in difficult discussions about how to use available resources to best serve students and meet the state's need for educated Californians."[1] Career technical education programs are generally more expensive to offer compared to solely lecture-based courses due to equipment acquisition and maintenance costs. Typically, external grant funds are utilized for initial program development and one-time equipment expenditures in alignment with federal and state procurement policies such as Education Department General Administrative Regulations (EDGAR), the Office of Management and Budget (OMB) circulars, and the California State Budget and Accounting Manual (SAM/BAM). In addition to a college's general fund, historically one of the most common sources for CTE equipment purchases and program support is the Carl D. Perkins Career and Technical Education Act (reauthorized for the fourth time in 2006 and commonly referred to as Perkins IV) whose authorization extended until 2014.

In a review of state and local district policies regarding the sale or disposition of equipment purchased through Perkins 1C funding, it was learned that existing policies cover the process of acquisition but nothing specifically on the disposition of said equipment except a common reference to federal policies.[2] When upgrading equipment or discontinuing a CTE program, most districts simply dispose of items in the landfill or sell equipment to the highest bidder (typically a scrap metal supplier), as allowed in California State Education Code §81450-81460. But the same Ed Code sections also allow local districts to exchange or donate instructional property to another public entity and that to maximize the State's investment in acquiring instructional equipment, local policies should require notice to other public educational entities for transfer prior to the surplus or sale of said equipment.[3] However, a central problem is that there is no effective mechanism for multiple colleges and multiple high schools to communicate with each other. One must make individual contact to ascertain if another institution has interest in receiving equipment that is no longer needed at their institution.

LABOR MARKET DATA

Other countries have stronger ties between the educational system and the occupational structure within their workforce. In the United States, the linkages seem to be contingent upon individual personalities, relationships, and an institution's dedication to ensuring CTE programs remain relevant to their regional economy. The California Community College system does require new programs to demonstrate local labor market demand as part of the new program approval process.[4] In fact, among the 21 required elements of the new for-credit program application, five are focused on demonstrating industry need for new CTE programs via regional quantitative data and/or documented industry need (required by CA Education Code §55130 and §78015). Quantitative data is typically obtained from the California Labor Market Information Division of the Employment Development Department which provides industry and occupational counts, projections, and wages at the county or Metropolitan Statistical Area level. These employment statistics are based on economic models and thus the accuracy of their projections do not account for political, qualitative, or other variables that may affect regional employment need in the short-term. According to their publications, the CCCCO requirement for documented industry need can be satisfied by letters of support/commitment from local employers to hire program completers, a local survey of firms, and/or industry advisory committee minutes documenting those in attendance and their comments.[5]

California Education Code § 55601 also requires that CTE programs hold local industry advisory board meetings to review CTE curriculum and act as a liaison between the college/district and potential employers. Occasionally, California's Centers of Excellence (coeccc.net) will host industry panels/ webinars and/or produce environmental scan reports which contain relevant occupational data and qualitative industry needs. Labor market need is also captured by statewide industry advisory committees funded from Perkins IV representing specific industry sector areas.

FEDERAL WORKFORCE LEGISLATION

As aforementioned, many pieces of federal legislation support community colleges generally, and career technical education specifically, including the Morrill Act of 1862, the Smith-Hughes Act of 1917, the Carl D. Perkins Career and Technical Education Improvement Act of 2006 (called Perkins IV), the School to work Opportunities Act, and the Workforce Investment Act of 1998 renamed and reauthorized in 2014 as the Workforce Innovation and Opportunity Act. From 1862 to 1963, federal policy focused on expanding capacity and improving CTE programs to serve the needs of business and industry. From 1963 to the present, researchers assert that federal policy continues to support the improvement of CTE programs to prepare people for work, and an additional focus has emerged to increase access to those most in need: non-traditional students and special populations.[6]

Interestingly, most federal legislation up until 1998 defined vocational education, for the purpose of receiving federal funds, as preparation for occupations requiring other than a baccalaureate or advanced degree. In recognizing the growing economic importance to students and employers of lifelong learning and continuing education, the federal government today emphasizes using federal CTE funds more broadly to support state and local efforts to develop challenging academic CTE standards, integrating general education and CTE instruction, creating CTE pathways via articulation, and creating stronger linkages between secondary and postsecondary education.[7]

The reauthorization of Perkins IV takes a substantial leap forward from previous versions in encouraging high school courses in career-focused programs of study to articulate to postsecondary options. These 2+2 pathways are designed to promote, "services and activities that integrate rigorous and challenging academic and career and technical instruction, and that link secondary education and postsecondary education."[8] As a result, the integration within CTE has already begun and community college CTE programs are no longer merely a path directly into the labor market, but also a path to higher degrees. Over 70% of high school CTE students eventually pursue some postsecondary schooling, breaking the old vocational stereotype and further positioning CTE as a viable path towards further education as well as career preparation.[9] Similar financial incentives (e.g. Tech Prep grants and SB-70 funds) continue to result in a tighter coupling between general academics and career preparation at both the high school and community college levels. Published in many articles and research reports, the federal government continues to reaffirm their belief in CTE through an understanding that the security and welfare of a nation is directly contingent upon its ability to educate its citizenry for meaningful and productive work.

STATE POLICY INFLUENCES

It is well documented that the California Community Colleges are the most heavily regulated educational entity in the world. Since 1907, a piece-meal approach to its guiding legislation has slowly but consistently added statutes and regulations governing the functions of the community colleges. The cumulative effect of all these laws is mind-boggling. Nussbaum reports that in the California Education Code alone, there are over 2,200 statutes which directly regulate and affect the affairs of community colleges.[10] This is in addition to the more than 600 regulations adopted by the Board of Governors, the hundreds upon hundreds of federal statues and funding requirements—not to mention the local county, city, and governing board administrative regulations.

As of 1985, research conducted by the California Community College's Chancellor's Office concluded that the colleges were then governed by over 3,000 laws and statutes. This is in comparison to 250 statutes within the University of California system and 450 regulating the California State University system. In comparison to other state community college systems, Nussbaum asserts that California still far exceeds the other five largest community college systems: Illinois (275 statutes), Oregon (200 statutes), Michigan (200 statutes), New Jersey (175 statutes), and Florida (125 statutes).[11] All other state community college systems have even fewer laws regulating their operation. In the future, CTE professionals should be involved when additional educational policy is constructed to ensure that policy makers address the current educational issues and workforce trends based on research.

NOTES

1. Shulock, N., Offenstein, J., and Esch, C. (2011). *Dollars and Sense: Analysis of Spending and Revenue Patterns to Inform Fiscal Planning for California Higher Education*. Sacramento, CA: Institute for Higher Education Leadership & Policy. And. Shulock, N., Moore, C., and Offenstein, J. (2011). *The Road Less Traveled: Realizing the Potential of Career Technical*

Education in the California Community Colleges. Sacramento, CA: Institute for Higher Education Leadership & Policy.

2. Haines, D. (October, 2011). *Perkins Equipment Regulations Compendium.* Compiled by the California Community College Chancellor's Office Perkins 1B Statewide Advisory Committee for Industrial and Technical Education (CA grant #011-0162).

3. Ibid.

4. CCCCO. (2013). *Program and Course Approval Handbook, Fifth Edition.* California Community College Chancellor's Office.

5. Ibid.

6. Joint Special Populations Advisory Committee (2008). *Meeting the Needs of Students from Special Populations in California's K-12/Adult and Community College Systems.* Retrieved on November 5, 2011 from http://www.jspac.org/what-is-jspac/jspac-position-paper.

7. Moore, C., & Shulock, N. (January, 2013). *State and System Policies Related to Career Technical Education: High School to Community College to Workplace Pathways–a working paper.* Sacramento, CA: Institute for Higher Education Leadership & Policy.

8. Carl D. Perkins Career and Technical Education Improvement Act of 2006, Pub. L. 109-270, Sec. 1(a), §120 Stat. 683 (2006).

9. Levesque, K., Laird, J., Hensley, E., Choy, S.P., Cataldi, E., & Hudson, L. (2008). *Career and technical education in the United States: 1990 to 2005* (NCES 2008-035). Washington, DC: National Centers for Educational Statistics.

10. Nussbaum, T. (November, 1992). *Too Much Law . . . Too Much Structure: Together We Can Cut the Gordian Knot.* Paper presented to the Community College League of California.

11. Ibid.

Chapter Three

Program Accretion and Program Discontinuance

This chapter provides a background on program development, program accretion, program discontinuance within higher education, and program discontinuance specifically within community colleges.

THE CALIFORNIA COMMUNITY COLLEGE PROGRAM APPROVAL PROCESS

The Conceptual Framework for Career and Technical Education asserts that CTE curriculum and program delivery are at the conceptual core of Career & Technical Education. As industries evolve, change practices, and as new technologies are introduced into the workplace, CTE programs must be created/revised to keep pace with industry advancements. The literature asserts that the need to revise/eliminate outdated curriculum and to develop new programs to meet the emerging needs of industry and society is a seemingly endless activity. Especially in fields where technology is constantly changing (e.g. Multimedia or Information Communication Technologies), as soon as a program begins to be offered in a given college catalog, faculty must seemingly start the revision process again. However, there is considerable variation across states in regards to the structure, policies, and procedures governing the approval of new, or revision of existing, postsecondary CTE programs.

Within California, the CTE program approval process for creating new CTE programs is documented in detail in the 249-page Program and Course Approval Handbook.[1] However, recent reports document that the current approval process for CTE programs, and the absence of effective processes to terminate low-priority programs, constrains the responsiveness of CTE curricula to changing labor market needs. There are different approval steps and processes depending on the type of CTE program being established. The process for approving local "Employment Concentration" certificates (defined as totaling less than 18 units) is much simpler than certificates totaling 18 units or more. As stated in the aforementioned "Labor Market Data" section, the new program application requires 21 elements to be submitted, five of which are specifically focused on demonstrating industry need for new CTE programs. But, this Handbook only documents the content required in the tangible application itself. It is the long duration and complicated approval process at the local level that is found by many faculty members to be cumbersome, and thus is often avoided.

Many community colleges (especially multi-college districts) have handbooks greater than 20 pages outlining the process for receiving new/revised program approval. Recently the CCC moved to a new online system for reviewing and approving courses/programs called CurricUNET. At the broadest sense there are four steps to moving new curricula through the process: 1) College & District, 2) Regional Consortium, 3) State Chancellor's Office, 4) ACCJC. But the details of shepherding new courses and programs through the approval process at the local level are far more complicated due to college-specific strategic planning workflows and approval trees based on the local college's organizational chart. In an attempt to provide the reader with some understanding of this process, while remaining germane to the research at hand, below is an outline of the process steps at one community college district in California. When not a single meeting or deadline is missed, this process takes 12 months—at best—from when a faculty has already developed the course content to when it can be offered to students. Most steps represents anywhere from 1–15 working days to complete since 5–10 days advanced notice is often needed prior to the next meeting to provide sufficient time for review and analysis.

1. Faculty member generates idea and begins research
2. New program is brought to Academic Senate for conceptual approval (first read)
3. New program is brought to Strategic Planning Council for conceptual approval (first read)
4. Industry input is received and documented via local Industry Advisory Board meeting (chronologically this could occur anytime during the first 6 steps)
5. New course(s) are created in CurricUNET including textbooks, sample assignments, student learning outcomes, etc.
6. New program is created in CurricUNET including description, course sequencing, program learning outcomes, etc.

7. Members from the discipline review and make comments (first read)
8. Any needed changes are made
9. The discipline votes on the new curriculum (second read)
10. The department then reviews and makes comments (first read)
11. Any needed changes are made
12. The department votes on the new curriculum (second read)
13. Department Chair approves curriculum in CurricUNET
14. Institutional Research reviews and approves
15. Library resource review and approval
16. Articulation Officer reviews and approves
17. CTE Dean/administrator has the option to review (no approval)
18. DSPS reviews and approves (if the proposal is for distance education)
19. The district's "technical review committee" reviews and approves
20. The college's Curriculum Committee reviews and makes comments (first read)
21. Any needed changes are made
22. The Curriculum Committee votes on the new curriculum (second read)
23. Regional Consortium (comprised of regional college CTE Deans meeting 6 times a year) review for regional impact/saturation (first read)
24. Any needed changes are made
25. The Regional Consortium votes on the new curriculum (second read)
26. College Vice President approves (resource impact)
27. New program is brought to Academic Senate for final approval (second read)
28. New program is brought to Strategic Planning Council for final approval (second read)
29. College President for review and approval
30. District Chancellor for review and approval (multi-college district)
31. District Strategic Planning Council as informational item (multi-college district)
32. District Curriculum Committee as informational item (multi-college district)
33. District Academic Senate as informational item (multi-college district)
34. Board of Trustees for final approval
35. Complete application with all signature pages and appendices (100+ pages) submitted to State Chancellor's Office for review approval
36. Any needed edits or clarifications are re-submitted
37. Substantial change Proposal is submitted to ACCJC
38. Finally, the new course and/or program can be added to the College Catalog to then be offered the subsequent term.

PROGRAM ACCRETION

In Hefferlin's book, *Dynamics of Academic Reform*, the process of program accretion is aptly described in the following statement,

> Rather than directly substituting the new for the old, the new is merely added-either as an elective course that may be taken in lieu of the old, or as a course in a new parallel degree program...conflicts are avoided by beginning separately and then only slowly allowing the new to be substituted for the old. [2]

Birnbaum echoes the reality that conflict is often avoided. [3] Since institutions of higher learning experience great inertia, educators often do not to eliminate existing curricula when adding new courses/programs. There is agreement that during times of rising revenue, many organizational and interpersonal conflicts are mediated by adding positions and resources rather than making difficult choices. [4] In their study of bureaucratic accretion in the University of California system, Gumport and Pusser confirm that constant bureaucratic growth occurs since public academic institutions are called to cultivate the stability of current offerings as well as initiate new innovations. [5]

The literature on program accretion seems to resound in a unifying voice regarding program and personnel growth. Hefferlin asserted that American multiversities have grown by absorbing, one by one, the programs and services once offered by specialized institutions, further causing academic accretion. [6] In calculating all types of academic reforms (new courses, course modifications, or course deletions), Hefferlin cited some state colleges growing the number of undergraduates courses by 53% over a 5-year period due to new knowledge, increased specializations, the growth of the faculty ranks, the adoption of independent study, and vocational course offerings with a more narrowed focus. [7]

Metzger's historical analysis of changes within academia demonstrates that curricular changes, when viewed longitudinally, highlight different types of accretion. [8] He emphasized the importance of academic specialization as it is formally organized in university faculty and program offerings over a period of time. Metzger's work was significant in explaining the various ways in which program specialization is likely to occur: 1) subject parturition, in which subspecialties are birthed from more inclusive subjects; 2) program affiliation, in which new academic programs are created to accommodate new professions or emerging fields; and 3) subject dignification, in which previously marginalized subjects gain legitimacy in academia. Metzger makes distinctions among different types of growth by specialization and this implies that when the opposite occurs, namely program discontinuance, programs may similarly do so in various configurations (e.g. by absorbing subspecialties, combining inclusive subjects, and/or delegitimizing certain subjects).

PROGRAM VITALITY & DISCONTINUANCE POLICIES

In order to properly understand the status of CTE program discontinuance throughout community colleges in California, this research first needed to identify if all 72 districts had a current board policy in place to guide the review and termination of academic programs (often called Program Vitality & Discontinuance, or Program Discontinuance).

Although having a PD policy is required in California Education Code §51022, only 60 of 72 community college districts currently have an approved PD policy. A few faculty members have anecdotally shared they feel these policies are not properly structured and thus some colleges may not be deleting outdated or unoffered CTE programs from their catalog. The result of absent or ineffective PD policies could be that some community colleges may be offering low-enrolled, low-priority, and/or outdated programs of study. Other colleges may have programs listed in the catalog that have not been offered for years thus confusing students as to the college's actual offerings which could negatively impact student success. Some colleges provide a laundry list of possible elective courses within a given program in the printed catalog, but in reality only offer the minimum number of courses for students to complete the certificate/degree without any real options of coursework variability.

UNIVERSITY PROGRAM DISCONTINUANCE

Although not a vast body of knowledge, previous research does discuss program termination (academic retrenchment) at the university level. Philosophically, Clark[9] and Kerr[10] discuss the organizational system of higher education and its ability to add and eliminate subjects based on shifting intellectual pursuits. Replacement theories also outline the need to eliminate a program when something new is added.[11] Hefferlin cites that some courses are often abandoned through attrition if their content ceases to be relevant, or it is consolidated from discrete fields into broader areas.[12] Case studies have also been conducted looking at university program and departmental accretion over time.[13]

Gumport & Snydman assert that changing economic conditions and enrollment fluctuations often pressure university leaders to select those endeavors worthy of continued investment, resulting in the weeding out of obsolete units and pruning of disciplines that have grown excessively.[14] Their distinction between the programmatic structure and the bureaucratic structure of an institution is central to their discussion. University-wide committees are often charged with planning, mission, resource allocation, and personnel decisions which tend to affect the bureaucratic structure via the addition or deletion of departments and divisions. Whereas, the authors assert the programmatic structure of academic offerings tend to require faculty approval from curriculum committees and/or academic senates. Thus they caution examining separately the organizational changes of the programmatic structure versus the bureaucratic structure. This is an important distinction helping to focus the present research on the programmatic structure of academic CTE offerings.

Curriculum and organizational restructuring creates political tensions between faculty members and administrators. Gumport writes, "Retrenchment entails difficult value-laden, long-range decisions about the social functions and purposes of higher education, including what will constitute legitimate academic knowledge, academic vocations, and knowledge products."[15] Her exploratory investigation drew from case study research at two research universities in which she conducted semi-structured interviews with faculty and administrators. Gumport documents the processes (or lack thereof) many universities engaged in to determine "which programs are essential, and which are less essential."[16] For example, one institution attempted to differentiate quality programs from others by measuring full-time equivalent data, research grant awards, and faculty publication counts only to later acknowledge that quantitative measures were not accurate because of the many "anointed programs" (such as Business and English) that could not be eliminated regardless of the data. While some of Gumport's research focuses on the elimination and merging of departments and disciplines rather than specific program evaluation processes, the political lens within an economic context that she discusses is extremely relevant to the contemporary retrenchment struggles within the CCC system. Her research suggests that perhaps both quantitative metrics as well as qualitative/political factors should be taken into account within program discontinuance procedures, but cautions that the political influences may trump rational decision making processes.

Hefferlin's writings on academic reform focused more specifically on the deletion, expansion and specialization of the curriculum.[17] Hefferlin looked at individual courses in departments that were completely removed or those folded-in or merged within related departments. His theory states that while the expansion of course offerings tends to happen during flush economic and political periods, the reform of existing academic curriculum most often occurred during times of instability and vulnerability. Times of chaos, uncertainly, or economic upheaval tend to produce innovative and otherwise unthinkable contractions and deletions of academic programs. This correlation between the likelihood of program discontinuance and external economic factors is very important in understanding the conditions within which a

given academic structure may be altered; such as during the present economic climate and resource-starved community college systems.

One documented area of the perception of community college program
deletion/discontinuance includes surveys of college presidents and their perception of course/program development and deletion. In a study sponsored
by the American Council on Education, two-thirds of presidents felt they had
limited involvement in course development/revision, however almost eighty
percent cited being very much involved in course/program deletion.[18] Politically and intellectually, this research suggests that faculty spearhead course
development, but the top administration spearheads program discontinuance.
Of course, as a result of shared governance legislation in states like California, the curriculum is primarily a faculty responsibility and not solely under
the academic administrative purview.

COMMUNITY COLLEGE PROGRAM DISCONTINUANCE

Although academic research is almost silent on the issue of community college program discontinuance, there are four sections of California Education
Code that provide guidance in this area. The first section, §70902(b), bestows
power to each locally-elected board to establish policies and approve courses
of instruction and educational programs. Similarly, section §55130 grants
each Chancellor the authority to determine if an educational program should
no longer be offered as well as specifying the effective date of termination.
The third relevant section, §51022 requires community college district
boards to approve policies, "for the establishment, modification, or discontinuance of courses or programs. Such policies shall incorporate statutory
responsibilities regarding vocational or occupational training program review
as specified in section §78016 of the Education Code."

The fourth relevant CA Educational Code section, §78016, requires that
CTE programs are reviewed every two years to ensure that each program a)
meets labor market demand, b) does not represent unnecessary duplication of
other manpower training programs in the area, and c) is of demonstrated
effectiveness as measured by the employment and completion success of its
students. This section further states that CTE programs not meeting these
criteria "shall be terminated within one year." Although this termination
deadline is approved Education Code, anecdotally PD does not consistently
occur within a year, and district PD policies allowing a longer discontinuance
timeline may be in conflict with this law.

In addition to these state laws, the Accrediting Commission for Community and Junior Colleges (ACCJC) Standard II.A.6.b states, "When programs
are eliminated or program requirements are significantly changed, the institution makes appropriate arrangements so that enrolled students may complete

their education in a timely manner with a minimum of disruption." Although not a legislative mandate, the accreditation standards are influential and help to ensure colleges maintain operating practices that support student learning. By specifically obligating a college to meet the needs of enrolled students, this standard implies that colleges should have policies in place which address the elimination of programs.[19] Moreover, college faculty members and administrators should discuss how students are informed about how to complete the educational requirements for a program that is discontinued or significantly modified.[20]

The only other document I could find referencing community college PD is a California Academic Senate white paper published in 1998 (and revisited in 2012) discussing the faculty perspective on program discontinuance.[21] The initial white paper reviewed education code (same as relevant today), collective bargaining concerns, budget concerns, and discussed the need for balancing the college curriculum. Although it was not quantified, the authors state that many districts then did not have a policy for program discontinuance and many singular approaches used were inconsistent. The 1998 paper called for districts to consult collegially with academic senates in establishing said policies and it made recommendations to modify the language in the aforementioned sections of education code to ensure effective faculty participation in the discontinuation process.

The 2012 revision of this white paper affirmed that many districts still do not have program discontinuance policies in place and thus, "programs have been terminated using inconsistent approaches, which is problematic for students, counselors, and academic senates, each of whom feels significant repercussions when discontinuance is managed inconsistently."[22] The Academic Senate also documents the introduction of the terms *program vitality* and *program viability* as interchangeable substitutes for program discontinuance in many district policies. After outlining many different facets of the PD process and providing examples, the Academic Senate 1) observes that no universally accepted definition of, or criteria for, evaluating academic programs exists, and 2) reaffirms that program discontinuance should be constructed and implemented separately from program review processes.[23]

Other than these Education Code sections, the accreditation standard, and these Academic Senate white papers, academic research is silent specifically on community college program discontinuance...until now.

NOTES

1. CCCCO. (2013). *Program and Course Approval Handbook, Fifth Edition.* California Community College Chancellor's Office.

2. Hefferlin, J. B. L. (1969). *Dynamics of Academic Reform.* San Francisco, CA: Jossey-Bass, p. 29.

3. Birnbaum, R. (1989). *How Colleges Work: The Cybernetics of Academic Organization and Leadership*. San Francisco, CA: Jossey-Bass Publishers.

4. Gumport, P., and Pusser, B. (1995). A Case of Bureaucratic Accretion: Context and Consequences. *The Journal of Higher Education*, Vol. 66, No 5, pp. 493–520.

5. Ibid.

6. Hefferlin, J. B. L. (1969). *Dynamics of Academic Reform*. San Francisco, CA: Jossey-Bass.

7. Ibid.

8. Metzger, W. (1987). "The academic profession in the United States." In B. Clark (Ed.). *The Academic Profession* (pp. 123–208). Berkeley, CA: University of California Press.

9. Clark, B. R. (1983). *The higher education system: Academic organization in cross-national perspective*. Berkeley, CA: University of California Press.

10. Kerr, C. (1987). A critical age in the university world: Accumulated heritage versus modern imperatives. *European Journal of Education*, 22(2), pp. 183–193.

11. Levine, A. (1997). How the academic profession is changing. *Daedalus*, 126(4), p. 1–20. And: Massy, W. (1996). *Resource allocation in higher education*. Ann Arbor, MI: University of Michigan Press.

12. Hefferlin, J. B. L. (1969). *Dynamics of Academic Reform*. San Francisco, CA: Jossey-Bass.

13. Gumport, P., and Snydman, S. (2002). The Formal Organization of Knowledge: An Analysis of Academic Structure. *Journal of Higher Education*, Vol 73, No 3, pp 375–408.

14. Ibid.

15. Gumport, P. (1993). The Contested Terrain of Academic Program Reduction. *The Journal of Higher Education*, Vol. 64, No. 3, Retrenchment, pp. 283–311.

16. Ibid. p. 291.

17. Hefferlin, J. B. L. (1969). *Dynamics of Academic Reform*. San Francisco, CA: Jossey-Bass.

18. Eaton, J. (1992). Presidents and Curriculum. National Center for Academic Achievement & Transfer, 3(8). American Council on Education.

19. Academic Senate for California Community Colleges (Fall, 2012). *Program Discontinuance: A Faculty Perspective Revisited*.

20. Ibid.

21. Academic Senate for California Community Colleges (Fall, 2012). *Program Discontinuance: A Faculty Perspective Revisited*. And: Academic Senate for California Community Colleges (Spring, 1998). *Program Discontinuance: A Faculty Perspective*.

22. Academic Senate for California Community Colleges (Fall, 2012). *Program Discontinuance: A Faculty Perspective Revisited*, p. 5–6.

23. Ibid.

Chapter Four

From the Field

PD at Three Community Colleges

During the course of studying program discontinuance at three different community colleges, a total of 34 study participants took part in the interview sessions (a 70.45% response rate). The average duration of these interviews was 48 minutes. Fifteen interviews (44%) were conducted face-to-face. Due to difficulty in aligning schedules and/or geographical proximity, the remaining nineteen interviews were conducted over the telephone. An extensive review of multiple sources including document and archival records occurred for each institution, on-site and/or remotely. This chapter includes the results from the document analysis and interview results from the three institutions included in this research.

COMMUNITY COLLEGE A

College A is a two-year community college located in Southern California, is part of a multi-college district, and is accredited by the Accrediting Commission for Community and Junior Colleges of the Western Association of Schools and Colleges. The college offers a wide variety of CTE programs as well as general education and transfer degree options (over 45 in total). College A provides education and services to over 16,000 students annually; over 60% of whom are part-time students. This case included ten interviews with faculty and administrators, review of germane documentation (catalogs, class schedules, college website, meeting minutes, power point presentations, completed program reviews, board of trustee minutes, reports, and memos), and archival research (historical listings of programs, program impact data analysis, college demographic data, Board policy for program discontinuance, and published reports).

Recent Program Discontinuation Process

In 2007, College A sought to create a 5–7 year master plan to ensure its CTE departments, programs, and certificates were aligned with the needs of its local community. A local taskforce was created to review existing CTE program data, reports, labor market information, industry scans, and other pertinent information. This ad hoc taskforce recommended modifications to the college's portfolio of CTE programs; specifically recommending the college should offer fewer programs, but spend the time and resources to make those programs best-in-class. The college's administration further supported the effort in 2008 by hiring external consultants to review the composition, program review, workforce requirements, and success metrics of all career & technical education programs. The consultants identified nine CTE programs that were in need of reorganization or retirement, and proposed possible synergies via combining multiple programs.

The subsequent year, College A formed multiple working groups to create reorganization/transition plans which included curriculum changes, departmental reassignments, and communications to students. Identified programs were put through the college's program discontinuation process. Five CTE programs were merged into two programs causing a few faculty members to transfer into a separate department; three other programs were discontinued (two, in part, due to faculty retirements). Fiscal and human resources were reallocated thus enabling other programs to grow/strengthen. The archival analysis confirmed that these merged/discontinued programs were reflected in the college's printed catalog of offerings. As a result of the multiple curriculum changes, the number of programs printed in the college catalog decreased, but the number of fulltime equivalent students (FTES) was maintained, and the number of program completions increased.

Process Catalyst and/or Influential Individuals

College A engages in a Program Vitality review process for all CTE programs every two years. A Dean or faculty member can then recommend a program for an "extended review" process if additional resources or potential discontinuance is recommended. If multiple programs are identified to undertake an extended review process, the Vice President decides which three will undergo review that year. (It is a capacity constraint to process more than three each year). Along with enrollment figures and the program's cost, curriculum that has not been updated (and thus may be perceived as outdated) are significant variables under consideration during the extended review process. In addition, the case study interviews revealed that fiscal constraints resulting from the state economy, new academic administration leadership, a program viability report, and the perception that the college offered too many programs, were all convergent factors that intersected simultaneously to result in multiple program discontinuance processes. The academic Deans, Academic Senate leadership, and Chief Instructional Officer were the most influential individuals during College A's discontinuance processes.

The Role of Policy

College A seemingly followed their Board Policy and Program Vitality review process for all CTE programs, although the duration of the process was elongated beyond the policy's stated timeline. Many interviewees commented on the extremely long time it took from beginning to end (almost 3 years) instead of the stated policy's one year deadline. The college's Program Vitality process is distinctly separate from Program Review, although the former is a connected result of the later. External consultant recommendations (not part of the policy) heavily influenced the college's process and program identification. The college president ultimately communicates the final decision to the college community via a letter with complete background and explanation, in alignment with their policy.

The Impact of Culture

Multiple individuals interviewed claimed that the culture at College A was typically relaxing and positive, using adjectives such as amazing, law-abiding, and collaborative. But, while engaged in the program discontinuance process the culture was described by some as vindictive, contentious, and intimidating, resulting in a perceived adversarial faculty versus administration culture. Although better at the time of this research, the overall culture was described as having, "a tendency to go up and down in our willingness to work together and willingness to fight. We are working well together now, but a year ago it would have been a disaster." Akin to the chicken-or-egg primacy question, the program discontinuance process was affected by the culture at College A, and the culture was seemingly affected by the program discontinuance process.

The PD process itself was unilaterally described as too long, resulting in a contentious and adversarial culture. One employee commented, "we should have ripped the band-aid off fast and dealt with issues later on instead of letting issues simmer for almost three years." From more than one person's perspective, this institution's inclusive culture and desire to ensure everyone was heard ended up elongating the process and arguably thus causing more pain. As another interviewee described it, "some decisions should have been made quicker...you don't tell people you'll get back to them in a month. There were delays in decisions, probably for really good reasons, but that was problematic."

Feelings and Perceptions

Transferring programs and faculty between academic departments/disciplines was perceived by some involved to be a transfer (gain or loss) of both human and fiscal resources and consequently leveraging power within the institution. Managing this change at College A both threatened and permanently strained many relationships. Even though the process, data analysis, external consultants, and internal working groups all agreed with the course of action, the sound structural process could not prevent hurt feelings, lingering resentment, and political infighting. On faculty member stated, "So, on paper it all made a great deal of logical sense, but in dealing with human beings it isn't always logical. There are still bad feelings about it." In fact, more than one individual refused to participate in this research study citing negative feelings towards the outcome of the process as a reason for declining.

Conversely, the final results of the program discontinuance processes were positively perceived by a number of individuals. Their process resulted in a number of positive solutions that helped struggling programs get the direction and support needed to improve. One interviewee stated, "[It] worked for some but not for others...the process objectively worked for the institution because students are completing and getting jobs which is our job in CTE. So whether or not it worked for one faculty or not doesn't matter...it works for the students." Another interviewee stated that the members of the ad hoc committee were trying to be as neutral as possible and really wanted to help programs to make them stronger. After reviewing all the archival evidence, documents and policies, and the case study interviews, it appears that this institution had a very strong process, but the implementation of that process caused some very mixed feelings and perceptions.

College A Summary

The program discontinuance process at College A resulted in five CTE programs merged into two programs, and three other programs were discontinued. Fiscal and human resources were reallocated thus enabling other programs to grow/strengthen evidenced by enrollment growth. The archival analysis confirmed that these merged/discontinued programs were reflected in the college's printed catalog of offerings the subsequent year. As a result of the multiple curriculum changes, the total number of programs printed in the college catalog decreased, but the number of fulltime equivalent students (FTES) maintained while the number of program completions increased.

As mentioned, the PD process itself was unilaterally described as too long, resulting in a contentious and adversarial culture. Timelines within the process were either elongated, or not followed, thus stretching out the process duration longer than necessary. Even though the process, data analysis, external consultants, and internal working groups all agreed with the course of action, the sound structural process could not prevent hurt feelings, lingering resentment, and political infighting for resources.

COMMUNITY COLLEGE B

College B is located in Southern California, is a two-year community college within a multi-college district, and is accredited by the Accrediting Commission for Community and Junior Colleges of the Western Association of Schools and Colleges. The college offers two semesters throughout the year (Fall and Spring) in addition to a summer session (May through August) serving approximately 15,000 students. College B's offerings includes lower division preparation in a wide variety of transfer majors for the baccalaureate degree, programs which lead to associate degrees and certificates of achievement, and numerous occupational majors in areas geared to local and national employment needs/trends. This case included twelve interviews with faculty and administrators, review of germane documentation (catalogs, class schedules, meeting minutes, completed program review templates, board of trustee minutes, program viability reports, and internal memos), and archival research (administrative procedural manual, historical listings of programs, power point presentations, college demographic data, Board policy for program discontinuance, CTE program reports, and internal emails).

Recent Program Discontinuation Process

In the last three academic years, College B has considered seven academic CTE programs for program discontinuance (along with other non-CTE and non-academic programs). As a result of their process, six of these CTE programs were discontinued (although two of these retained their discipline and selected courses which also serve other programs and/or transfer goals), one fulltime faculty left the institution, and a number of part-time faculty members were subsequently no longer hired to teach. This all occurred after a lengthy and significant revision to the district's PD policy and local college processes.

Process Catalyst and/or Influential Individuals

College B's PD process is connected to their annual program review process which serves as the catalyst for the program discontinuance committee to meet. During the program review, each metric is evaluated and ranked as either high, medium, or low. The program review committee then recommends that the program remains stable, is reduced, is provided resources to be strengthened, or is to be reviewed for discontinuance. If the latter is chosen, pending presidential approval, a separate ad hoc committee is then formed (thus a separate but related process begins) and an expanded list of metrics are then further reviewed by a separate group. Throughout this process, the total operational costs of the program are not included in the annual program review process, although they were reviewed by the subsequent ad hoc PD committee. Due to the strong link between PD and the program review process, one interviewee commented that, "the criteria established drove the process." Key individuals included the executive cabinet (especially President, Chief Instructional Officer, and Chief Financial Officer), academic senate president, selected deans, and the program review committee.

The Role of Policy

College B follows an approved district board policy for both program review (including their evaluation rubric) and their program discontinuance process. In board policy, College B's program review process is linked to the program discontinuance process. As mentioned by one interviewee, the program review process is perceived as a preamble to the administrative procedure 4021 for program discontinuance. Previously contentious and unhelpful, the board policy was revised within the last 5 years and is now perceived to be a good guide for the college to follow. The district PD process now includes an analysis of program metrics followed by a recommendation by an ad hoc committee, then subsequent Academic Senate and administrative reviews. The same PD evaluation rubric is used for CTE, non-CTE, and even student services programs. As a result of the link between program review and program discontinuance, one interviewee stated, "Where I see some of the after math coming is that now people see they need to take their program plans more seriously, cause they see that it actually means something. You could write something and it never mattered; now it matters." Although the revised policy provides step-by-step process instructions, one interviewee also noted that, "some subjectivity exists as to if programs move forward past stage [X] or not." The average duration of their PD process used to be 2–4 years, but after significant revisions the process now takes a single semester (plus board action).

The Impact of Culture

The culture at College B significantly impacted the way the PD process had been developed. College B demonstrated a very collegial and inclusive culture. Faculty members took ownership of the PD policy revision process and choose to actively lead/engage it instead of "letting it happen to us." College B was also proudly described as having a very transfer-oriented academic culture; so many of the CTE programs (referred to as "professional CTE" programs as opposed to "traditional CTE") were designed for students to also transfer. The traditional CTE programs were "looked down upon." However, this dual laddering process unfortunately led to the easier discontinuation of CTE programs that only prepared students for gainful employment as those programs were perceived to only fill one of the two intended purposes (and not transfer). In at least one instance, no CTE representation was on the ad hoc committee reviewing CTE program vitality. Thus, CTE programs deemed viable to offer as for-credit offerings at other colleges were relegated to adult education offerings within this district.

College B espouses they have a dialog-rich culture with a "no surprises" ideology. The institution was also cited by one interviewee as, "notorious for our collaborative culture because the college was started by hippies with a thrust of consensus building. There is a lot of dialog, collaboration, and trust even if people are unhappy. Everyone gets to say their piece in a clear, laid-out process." Another stated that, "we talk to each other until someone agrees or they drop dead." This was echoed in the statement, "We are a college of conversation...We talk about it until everyone shuts up." Another passionately stated,

> Our campus is very rare. We're a family. Everyone really looks out for, likes each other, wants the best for each other, so any program discontinuance process is with everyone backing everyone else up. Our culture is very professional and we are very concerned about each other as colleagues and friends.

Yet another employee at College B cited that the culture, "tries to be very family, but I find it to be very forced." The PD process did result in strained relationships within their campus culture, but seemingly everyone at least understood the "why" behind the need to engage in the process.

Of note is that the PD process is significantly impacted if the institution is housed within a multi-college district given that the board policy is a shared one. Only at the local level may the institutional culture have an impact on the "how" of policy implementation, but not the "what." Issues or perspectives at one college have a direct affect at others. As one faculty member from College B stated referencing one of their sister colleges, "their chaos spilled over into us."

Feelings and Perceptions

Even in the midst of a statewide economic crisis, College B successfully separated the fiscal need to constrict its spending with the program discontinuance process. The overwhelming perception among those interviewed was that budget and fiscal availability did not cause the deletion of program offerings. It was stated that the budget crisis motivated the college to ensure they had a good policy in place (thus resulting in policy revisions a few years prior), but budget was not a sole or main catalyst in discontinuing CTE programs.

Since College B invests significant time meeting with each program lead/director every year to review unit plans (i.e. program review) most constituencies feel involved and heard in the process. But when a recommendation of "Review for Discontinuance" is selected by the review committee, it was reported that many faculty/directors then feel very defeated. One cannot ignore the psychological impact this outcome may have on an individual. One interview commented that this has one of two effects on the person: either a) they get very frustrated, mad, and potentially disengage (in one instance completely), or they get very motivated, charged up, and increase their output to strengthen and "save" their program.

College B Summary

As a result of their PD process, which is tightly coupled to their program review process, six of seven CTE programs under consideration were discontinued. The college's very transfer-oriented academic culture played a significant role in the tone, participation, and metrics used in evaluating CTE programs, occasionally without a strong CTE advocate involved. Following the first program discontinuance process that was described as chaotic and unorganized, the college's PD process was dramatically altered/improved for subsequent programs. College B's program review documents now play a stronger role in their overall PD process as a result of recent policy changes and the college culture has been altered to accept discontinuance as part of their nomenclature. Although in the middle of a statewide budget crisis, it is noteworthy that the overwhelming perception among those interviewed was that budget and fiscal availability did not cause the deletion of program offerings; rather the process was heavily data-guided based upon metrics stated in their written templates and PD policy.

COMMUNITY COLLEGE C

College C, located in central California, is a two-year community college serving as a single-college district, and is accredited by the Accrediting Commission for Community and Junior Colleges of the Western Association of Schools and Colleges. The college serves approximately 11,000 students at its main campus as well as via multiple satellite locations. College C offers general education and degrees, along with numerous CTE programs in focused areas of expertise in alignment with local labor market and community needs. This case included twelve interviews with faculty and administrators (80% response rate), review of germane documentation (college catalogs, class schedules, meeting minutes, board of trustee minutes, program analysis reports, and internal memos), and review of archival research (administrative procedural manual, historical listings of programs, college demographic data, Board policy for program discontinuance, and college-wide memos/emails).

Recent Program Discontinuation Process

The district's process outlined in AP 4021 was utilized during academic year 2011-12 for a full review of one CTE program. The completion of that procedure revealed in archival research that the process was effective for revitalization, but not for discontinuance, nor was it universally deemed expedient. As such, a one-time policy modification was proposed and approved in response to an immediate and forecasted budget reduction. Following the approval of that policy modification, the college reviewed and took action on 29 different academic and student service programs (of which 19 were academic CTE programs). The review of these 29 programs resulted in the discontinuance of 10 programs, suspension of 1 program, 6 programs retained, and 12 programs modified/reduced.

Process Catalyst and/or Influential Individuals

It is important to note that external to the institution both California Proposition 30 and the regional accreditation body (ACCJC) had an indirect influence which resulted in College C beginning the program discontinuance policy modification dialog/process initially. As one interview mentioned, "Receiving a fiscal stability sanction from accreditation was such a catalyst for change. It was a wake-up call. The college wasn't doing the work that needed to be done." Another similarly noted, "the college was in crisis-mode." Collectively, this perfect storm of fiscal stability sanctioning, the state budget crisis, the accretion of programs, new leadership, and neglected program review processes, seemingly forced the PD issue to the forefront.

According to district policy, any full-time faculty member in the program, division chair, dean, or the academic vice president may prepare a request and present it to the strategic governing committee for their approval to initiate the program discontinuance process (called the Program Revitalization, Suspension, and/or Discontinuance Process). However, during the one-time policy modification period, the academic affairs office created a list (in rank order by efficiency) of potential programs to be considered for discontinuance which totaled the bottom third of all programs offered (note: programs with an efficiency calculation 12 or less were heavily evaluated). Notification was sent to program chairs and affected faculty simultaneously with the list being presented to College C's strategic governance committee. The college president, vice president of business affairs, academic senate president, and the academic vice president were the most influential individuals during the modified policy period.

The Role of Policy

College C diligently adhered to Board Policy regarding program discontinuance during one full implementation cycle. The process steps consisted of a request to review a specific program, the review of the proposal by a college-wide committee, a program analysis completed by an ad hoc task force, recommendation (continuance, revitalization, suspension, or discontinuance), then final decision. Of particular note is that similarly to College B, the proposal request is informed by the college's program review process/ template. In a comprehensive manner, their policy contains a template for data analysis, process timelines, as well as the task force roles and responsibilities.

After completing an entire cycle, the college deemed the process lengthy and restrictive of nimbleness. One interviewee quipped, "we didn't' have the luxury of a long, drawn-out process." Thus, a one-time policy modification was approved by the college to review/reduce program offerings given current and forecasted available budget. Although the temporary policy modification was approved by the college strategic governance committee, the acceptance and appropriateness of this policy modification was not universally supported by interviewees. During a two-month duration, the modified process steps consisted of an ordered list of programs with reference data (quantitative & qualitative) to be created, then reviewed/ordered/ranked by a college-wide committee, an anonymous ranking vote, then a decision by the President in consultation with budget committee and fiscal impact analysis, and finally Board approval.

The Impact of Culture

Recently, the increased demands on everyone's job had reportedly created tension and a permeation of frantic hurriedness throughout the college culture. It was stated that "our culture is stressed out. The financial stress pushed us." One interviewee from College C articulately noted that, "We are in the human businesses. Accreditation has created so much work for folks that we spend less time just communicating, sharing, and being with one another. We're all so busy with our heads down, we don't have the opportunities to build trust and strengthen relationships. It really takes its toll on the campus climate." The institution had also experienced 6 presidents in 7 years, and many departments experienced a new Dean almost every year. The culture of the college shifted with the changes in leadership; this inconsistency was also stated to be a factor which resulted in numerous accreditation recommendations/sanctions. It was evident from case study research that the culture overall was not solid/strong or cohesive at the beginning of the process to "weather the storm" of PD successfully.

One research question in this study was to explore if college culture would have an impact on the PD process. But, more than the other two colleges researched, feelings were more overtly expressed about how the PD process had negatively impacted the culture at College C. For example, one employee commented:

> Describing the culture is a difficult question to answer. Perhaps distinctively proud; coming to the grips that they have an ACCJC sanction and that the finances of the colleges has progressed in such a way that it could not be what it was. They were coming to grips with ineffective leadership…it created an environment where there was some grudging acknowledgment that we needed to move to being a smaller school. The disagreement is that the administration will say we developed a fair and transparent system to move forward…and faculty will say a process was developed and it happened rather quickly without enough time for input and reflection.

In another example, when asked if their process was felt to have been effective, one employee commented, "you can plow through a bad process, but the carnage and wreckage we leave behind takes a long time to clean up and recreate the sense of community." Multiple staff stated that the culture is not as trusting as it used to be; some still question the motives of their colleagues.

However, a few interviewees did positively comment that the overall culture of College C was their professionalism and their family feel. For example, one stated that they "always felt that we were a family; but easier to talk with one another as we went through this process to explain reasonably why we were going through this process." There was an acknowledgement that the college was getting a little large to be a family, but that the general perspective was still there. It was observed that this, along with the unified goal of overcoming accreditation recommendations, is what helped get College C through the recent difficult budget period.

Feelings and Perceptions

Because the modified policy/process allowed for a list of academic programs to be identified first, with data analysis to follow, the perception by some interviewed was that the process "was fixed" to fit predetermined outcomes. There was also a certain amount of panic and urgency felt as a result of the expedited timeline established and heavy focus on fiscal impact. One inter-viewee noted that the college needed to give people the time and opportunity to be heard and to, "invest in them feeling that they were heard. Many are upset and hurt because they felt their voice wasn't heard. They were not given the opportunity they wanted to fight for their program. Talking for 3 minutes cannot defend a 10-year body of work; [it] doesn't value a decade of dedication to the college and the program. They would still be mad at you, but for different reasons." The dominant perception was that the modified process didn't give people enough time to be heard and validated. However, a few did note that the modified process did allow for all parties to be heard. One interviewee specifically stated that the process allowed for, "lots of input from the community to the deans and president when the list first became public; a lot of meetings with local industry."

Nevertheless, College C's program discontinuance process left hurt feel-ings and bitterness with some faculty contacted. Even though logically many understood why the process was occurring, and the dire fiscal situation in which College C found themselves, there was still a lingering perception that the leadership lacked thinking though the human element and was far too focused on budgetary impact. Overall, the recent process at College C seemed to result in low morale and feelings of distrust that will not soon be repaired.

College C Summary

As aforementioned, College C had experienced 6 presidents in 7 years, and many departments experienced a new Dean almost every year. The culture of the college shifted with the changes in leadership and this inconsistency was stated to be a factor which resulted in numerous accreditation recommenda-tions/sanctions. Collectively, this perfect storm of fiscal stability sanctioning, the state budget crisis, the accretion of programs, leadership turnover, and neglected program review processes, seemingly forced the PD issue to the forefront at College C, resulting in more discontinued programs in one term than anywhere else known in the state. As a result of their temporarily mod-ified PD process and external influencers, nine CTE programs under consid-eration were discontinued and another eight were significantly modified/ reduced (among other non-CTE programs). Looking further back, in 2011–2012 there were 199 certificate and degree offerings at College C. This was dramatically reduced to 126 offerings just two years later as evidenced in their 2013–2014 college catalog.

The PD process occurred rather quickly (just over two months, beginning to end) and seemingly drove a wedge further within the collaborative culture of the college leaving behind a trail of distrust and high anxiety. This case study research indicated that more attention could have been focused on the human resources frame and how people were going to feel valued throughout the process.

Chapter Five

Overarching Themes

While some unique differences existed at each college as previously described, some thematic patterns emerged in comparing interview responses which transcend individual college districts. In this chapter, I compare these convergent patterns leading to program discontinuance citing extensive quotations from case study interviewees. The quotes selected for publication align within the organizational frames as described by Bolman and Deal.[1]

HOW DID THE PROCESS OCCUR?

Given the timing of this case study research (2012–13) and the existing economic climate in the state of California, it is not surprising that budgetary issues repeatedly emerged in interviews as the catalyst for the PD processes to occur. Whether it was the applicability of categorical funding (aka Perkins IV) or the annual allocation reduction from Sacramento, available funding was either a direct or indirect factor in the merging/discontinuance of CTE programs. As mentioned previously, in one instance it was the overt variable triggering the PD process. Thus, this research concludes that budget was a significant factor considered in every PD process included in this study.

Without exception, the three community colleges that were the focus of this study followed written policies and procedures for triggering and completing program discontinuance processes. Although occasionally lengthened or expedited, each institution established and completed a documented process including ad hoc committees, data analysis, shared governance committees reviewing the findings, recommendations to college/district leadership, and approval by the Board of Trustees. The process initially occurred either through a systematic program review process (most often annually) and/or a targeted proposal/recommendation from a member of the college community (most often the academic administration). Of importance to note in this research is that each college's process was a little different. There was no uniform process discovered through this case study research. The culture and history of each institution had seemingly influenced and shaped their process. Also of note is that two of the three colleges included in this study were in the process of refining and further revising their PD processes at the time interviews were conducted. This indicates a process of sustained, continuous improvement where the process and policies are revisited and revised.

Also regarding the occurrences of the process, multiple interviewees stated that not having full-time faculty providing leadership to a specific program area indirectly put that CTE program on a path towards program discontinuance. "Those programs don't have a path, they just kind of sit there and aren't very supported," stated one faculty member. They continued, "Especially when local colleges have a stronger program that would serve them better." In addition to budgetary constraints and program review, the lack of dedicated faculty seemingly served as an indirect catalyst for many program discontinuance processes. One exception discovered was when a part-time faculty was paid a lead faculty stipend to provide leadership and guidance for a particular program/discipline (including such duties as student learning assessment reports, program review documents, etc.). Providing a part-time faculty member with such a stipend and role seemingly provided the CTE program with increased leadership, focus, and support.

While most institutions operationalized their board policy using entire academic programs (certificates or degrees) as the unit of analysis, one institution took a different approach and consciously separated out programs from courses and disciplines. The approach influenced not only how their process occurred, but the result of their review. Using these as three logically separate units of analysis, this institution is able to discontinue a program while still maintaining a discipline and increase section offerings of particular courses. In another instance, an academic program was retained but limited courses were maintained in their college catalog. Segmenting out program discontinuance, course discontinuance, and discipline discontinuance further expands the nomenclature within this research and requires PD college process and program review templates to have increased granularity.

HOW DID PEOPLE FEEL ABOUT THE PROCESS?

Taking into account Birnbaum's theory of procedural justice[2] and Bolman & Deal's human resource frame,[3] this research focused on the feelings, experiences, perceptions, and reactions of those directly involved in the PD process on each campus studied. It was discovered that what the process is called, and how the committee perceives their role, is very important. For example, initially at one institution researched some faculty members were struggling and wanted help to assist their program(s), but didn't know what to do. Allegedly their program review didn't directly help grow/strengthen a struggling program and the program discontinuance process had a negative connotation due to its title. So, the institution changed the name of the process (and all associated documents) to the Program Vitality process. The intention of the committee and the first step in the process became to help the program in any way the institution could, "in an ideal world" to improve. As reported during the case study research, "the process itself was consciously developed to find solutions and not to be punitive. We didn't want faculty to be afraid to recommend themselves, but instead to say, please help me." Only if the discovery process concluded that the program needed more than the college could provide, or if it was no longer viable regardless of size/impact, then it would be discontinued. This was validated by another interviewee's very poignant comment, "It is a miserable process, but I am incredibly proud of what we have achieved. Everyone was not happy. We fished out the ones that have a reason to exist and we protect them and nurture them and make them whole in a new refined version; and the ones that did not have a role at the moment were deleted." Yet another interviewee stated, "It can be hurtful for peers to hear others talk about their program…also don't want it to turn into lobbying or pandering to friends; the loudest shouldn't win, it should be based solely on data and their program review document, which carries a lot of the qualitative data into the process."

Another converging pattern discovered through this case study research that impacted people's feelings about the process was the composition of the ad hoc committee reviewing programs for discontinuance. Some institutions appoint the committee based on roles/titles; other institutions vote on who serves on the committee. At one college, the affected discipline faculty members were required to take part to provide anecdotal and qualitative information that may inform the committee. At this institution, discipline faculty were part of the entire dialog as well as the official vote determining the program's fate. Yet at another institution, the affected discipline faculty members were overtly and consciously omitted from the ad hoc process to ensure a non-biased and purely data-guided analysis. Only after the initial review were they invited to consult with the administration (twice; at different levels) regarding the committee's recommendation. At this second institution, it was felt that not having the discipline faculty in the room during the vote enables the committee to have more frank and honest dialog about the fate of the program without fear of mincing words or hurting the feelings of their colleague. However some faculty perceived this process as "bullying" and "never in the room when the decision was made."

Institutional culture greatly impacted the decision whether or not to include discipline faculty entirely, or just during a small advocacy component of the larger process, which had a direct impact on how people felt about their process. In both structures, however, different faculty members expressed not feeling heard. In their book, *Reframing Organizations: Artistry, Choice, and Leadership*, Bolman and Deal indicated that most all groups, institutions, and organizations encounter conflict.[4] The authors suggested this is because of differences in goals, perceptions, preferences, and beliefs. Faculty echoed this literature through their many comments about conflict during this study. One astutely observed that, "grumblings come from those not involved in the process; mainly from those that didn't check their e-mail." Additional quotes from those interviewed follow in later sections of this research organized by the theoretical framework's four frames.

According to the human resource frame, conflict arises not in vying for resources, but when the goals and needs of the organization are not congruous with the goals and needs of the person. Overall, no one interviewed enjoyed being engaged in a program discontinuance process, although most expressed an understanding as to why it needed to occur. One faculty called it a "necessary evil" commenting that it cannot be separated from the people involved and that no one wants to evaluate their colleagues' work or viability. But individuals felt better about the final outcome when the college administrators and Academic Senates laid out a rational and transparent process with frequent communication. Ensuring "many touches" occurred, such as an e-mail from the academic senate to affected faculty before the President's official memo to the community, helped people feel less threatened and to not feel assailed by others. Individuals also felt that they would not go back and do anything differently if they felt they had a voice during the process. There seemed to be a correlation between institutions that espouse a collaborative culture with those that had smooth PD processes.

ARE ACTUAL PROGRAMS OFFERED ALIGNED WITH THOSE PUBLISHED?

Some community colleges do not offer all the programs that are listed in their catalog or advertised in the state inventory.[5] Thus, I carried out a multi-year archival analysis of the actual program offerings versus those advertised and published. There was no marked variability in actual offerings compared to those published at the three colleges included in the research. There was an occasional one-year lag between removing deleted courses/programs from the printed catalog at two institutions, but this discrepancy was justified during the interviews as resulting from catalog printing deadlines which occurred just as the annual PD process was concluding. Thus, at some institutions the subsequent year's college catalog is approved/printed while the PD process is still being finalized. In another example, one college's official catalog listed 199 certificate and degree options the year before program discontinuance was initiated, and 126 offerings were listed two years after the PD processes concluded. While there may be some catalog listings that are not often scheduled, those colleges included in this case study did update their official catalogs either the very next year, or subsequent year, removing discontinued courses and programs from the official record.

WHAT IS THE ROLE OF POLICY IN PROGRAM DISCONTINUANCE?

There were a variety of opinions regarding even having a PD policy. More than one faculty member expressed that the mere existence of a policy enabled the administration to "do what they want." Where yet another faculty member mentioned that it was best for the faulty to "craft one's own destiny" and fully get involved with the development of the PD policy to ensure the decision would be made in a holistic manner. One faculty quipped, "The Academic Senate was so happy and proud of themselves for developing their own program discontinuance process…it ticked me off." In addition to the adherence to the local PD policy, the Academic Senate's rights (codified in California Assembly Bill 1725, also known as the 10 +1) were mentioned in a number of interviews noting that the role of policy was not exclusive to only college program discontinuance policies.

When asked about the role of policy, most commonly offered was the response, "I don't know." Even those faculty directly affected and/or in the thick of discussions about programs in their immediate area/department were unaware of (or at least did not recall) the Board policy for PD and if it was followed or not. However, when employees felt the process was successful it was because the policy focused on preventative measures and processes that systematically reviewed a program's vitality ever year or every two-years, not just the series of steps required to terminate a program offering.

Interestingly, one institution in this sample, College C, temporarily disregarded their Board policy (via official college committee vote) to meet dire fiscal circumstances and long-term fiscal/accreditation planning. The temporary modification to policy allowed the college to act swiftly, reviewing and discontinuing programs within two months, raising the question of the need/legitimacy for the policy's original timeline. In addition to policy modifications, this case study also raises the question of the title of the policy and the options that should result from the process. Namely, should the discontinuance process be distinctly separate from a revitalization process? For example, one employee mentioned in an interview that their institution "ended up keeping [program X] because other faculty were in an uncomfortable spot to kill it. So the policy was a suspension and revitalization process. By having those options as part of the process, it almost always guarantees the result as revitalization." A faculty member from a different institution stated, "Because our policy has a revitalization process to it, it was thought that program discontinuance would never happen." It seems apparent that the role of the policy, including its name and possible results/consequences, are of utmost importance to the overall PD process that a college district utilizes.

NOTES

1. Bolman, L. & Deal, T. (2008). *Reframing Organizations:* Artistry, Choice and Leadership. San Francisco: Jossey-Bass.

2. Birnbaum, R. (1989). *How Colleges Work: The Cybernetics of Academic Organization and Leadership*. San Francisco, CA: Jossey-Bass Publishers.

3. Bolman, L. & Deal, T. (2008). *Reframing Organizations:* Artistry, Choice and Leadership. San Francisco: Jossey-Bass.

4. Ibid.

5. Shulock, N., Moore, C., and Offenstein, J. (2011). *The Road Less Traveled: Realizing the Potential of Career Technical Education in the California Community Colleges*. Sacramento, CA: Institute for Higher Education Leadership & Policy.

Chapter Six

Convergent Patterns within the Four Frames

A significant element to a case study analysis is the review of the convergent patterns found within multiple cases. This section provides an overall summary of the common themes found within the three college case studies. The findings are organized by the four organizational frames (structural, human resource, political, and symbolic) as described by Bolman and Deal.[1] Selected quotations follow within each frame analysis to further illustrate the literal replication found within this research.

STRUCTURAL FRAME

Without exception, each of the colleges in this case study research relied heavily upon quantitative data metrics as a foundation for recommending a program for program discontinuance. While some of the specific formulas or weighting criteria differed, the structural frame was significantly at play during the beginning of every PD process analysis. Moreover, two of the three colleges included qualitative data in their initial program discontinuation evaluations. This included such items as the program's history, evolution, current status, root causes of perceived performance gaps, regional competition/collaboration, program demand and/or value added program components.

Some institutions adopted structural processes that logically enabled a smooth PD process. For example, one institution conducted their ad hoc committee vote anonymously via an online survey tool instead of openly during face-to-face meetings. Another institution annually scheduled 30 minute meetings with every single department/program (n=60+) each fall term in order to discuss their program review rubric and recommendation results. In this process, each program/department lead would meet with their Dean, Chief Instructional Officer, Institutional Researcher, Academic Senate President, and Chief Financial Officer to review/clarify their annual unit plan (program review). Although this process was described as "a real grind" it was also perceived as preventative in providing guidance and support ahead of time instead of "picking up the broken pieces" in a reactive mode. Such an annual structure also ensures regularity in process, equity amongst departments, and formal lines of communication, all of which are specifically recommended in the structural frame by Bolman & Deal.[2]

As aforementioned, high-cost CTE programs requiring fiscal resources and occasional additional funding (via grants and Perkins) were vulnerable to program discontinuance. More than one program was discontinued primarily due to the expense of the program in light of shrinking fiscal resources. One college made a point to acknowledge that even a revitalization plan would, "simply be too expensive." Fiscal analysis definitely played a role during CTE program discontinuations that occurred during the recent fiscal crisis (although two of the three colleges would uniformly verbalize that it was not the primary variable—the third college accepted and acknowledged the fiscal primacy of their decisions).

Adhering to external accreditation guidelines was also a significant factor in alignment with both the structural frame and program discontinuance policies. Both California's Proposition 30 and the regional accreditation body (ACCJC) had influenced more than one institution included in this case study to streamline/reduce their academic offerings. This influence from ACCJC universally came in the form of sanctions/recommendations where a college was out of compliance with fiscal long-term planning. Although Proposition 30 was passed by California voters increasing taxes to support, in part, higher education, had the legislation not passed all community colleges in the state would have needed to reduce budgets even further; thus most likely triggering more severe program discontinuance processes. This eventuality validates Hefferlin's theory of academic reform in that the reform of existing academic curricula most often occurred during times of instability and vulnerability.[3]

Without any prompting or discussion of the theoretical framework proposed for the present study, a number of interviewees made comments particularly relevant to the structural frame. Below are some selected comments organized by theme.

Some comments focused on specific elements of the PD process itself:

- "In order to make this work well, the tone and who leads, and structure of the recommending group is critically important. The [faculty] and the [administrator] led the meeting and spent a lot of time thinking about how to actually run that meeting, so that the people there knew they were doing a service to the college regardless of the decision, since you should constantly review programs and make decisions."

- "The process initially is rational, and then rationality gets thrown out the window. People have their minds made up. This is a political environment."
- "We did [recommend] programs and sent it to the President with full understanding that [they] could make modifications. [President] had to tell us in writing why some changes were made to the recommendations."
- "What you want is for there to be reasonable voices and the right people around the table. A process takes a few minutes to do it, but what makes it work is that way before that your governance system and understanding of roles and responsibilities needs to be so clear and sharp."
- "The PD process at [College] is analogous to a hiring committee…each stage is just about that one component (a paper screening, panel interview, then follow up questions in the 2nd level). The later stages add in other elements to consider."

Many others commented on the use of data and specific metrics utilized in making PD decisions:

- "There was a perception that the more efficient courses would thrive, but that has not manifested simply by eliminating low efficient classes. Students were both in the bread and butter as well as the low enrolled….some of those students just didn't come back."
- "Before the change, no one ever read the annual program reviews. One faculty slipped in a whole stack of blank paper and no one noticed. The campus was not really reviewing programs."
- "There is justification for lower efficiency within CTE programs, but still need to then look at certifications and graduates… Have to have a qualitative part with community need and labor market data."
- "The goal was if you have an opinion that a program should have been discontinued years ago, you are not allowed to have that opinion during this process. The people on the committee are chosen who have no axe to grind and no knowledge of the program—meant to be independent and objective. No one from the department present. It was so impressive; data provided for each program. Very strict rules about what you could say or couldn't. No second-hand knowledge of things you were told from the faculty/department. Only allowed to work from the paper. A real account to take out people. Looking just at the data… strategically about the data, not the people."

- "The focus had to do with efficiency. A term that never really crept up until recently. Programs [X] and [Y] had low efficiency and thus ended up on the list."
- "I didn't arm myself well with labor market data to educate people. Seemed common sense to me, but didn't grab the data in time."
- "There is always going to be toes stepped on and people don't like change or cuts in any area. No one wants things to happen to us; but whenever the statistical information can be brought in would be way more understandable to show data that could indicate decline or lack of fill rate or success. It's more palatable when data is there to support the recommendation instead of just saying, your area is too expensive."
- "I've been faculty for [X] years and told students not to complete, but to just get what they needed to then transfer. 18 of our degree units didn't even transfer. Can't get a job without a BA anyway. No completers up until this past year. Completers never were important before; the emphasis before was productivity and efficiency."
- "Our criteria looked at the weakest programs, not bad ones, with a low student-faculty ratio, with high overhead costs, or those with low student enrollment."
- "Our CTE students go to Skills USA and are national champions; we always medal. But that's not included in the metrics of the program discontinuance process, so it was very painful to cut CTE programs."
- "Making decisions based on inadequate full-time faculty is a bad policy. If you have tenured-track faculty that are unsuccessful, it makes it difficult on successful faculty and creates difficult faculty working conditions....they [successful faculty] have to make up the difference. It was not a stated variable, but definitely the less-performing faculty played a role in the closing of the program."

Others commented on the actual PD policy:

- "Policy was really long. The more people on the task force, the harder it is to schedule a time to meet, so that draws it out."
- "I've worked at [X] different colleges. This is the first one where the process is in place and the policy is being used."

A few comments focused on historical program accretion:

- "We grew with no control, and the college did not reign in programs over the years as it should have."
- "For a long time, we were inward looking, but not very deeply, which allows for programs to sprawl and not have a lot of critical examination."

- "It is better to merge programs together during tough times….We had so many programs that just developed along the years, and then budgets were not able to cover all that, and some of these programs have very high cost."

Some commented on the impact/affect from other neighboring institutions:

- "I was very particular in the cost-benefit analysis of staying … making a distinctive difference between [neighboring college's] program and ours."
- "Should we have a weak [X] program when [College Y's] program down the road is better?"

Others commented on their college's fiscal stability and strategic planning:

- "We seem to be more concerned on economics; that drives everything, not common sense or business sense. Purely on government legislation. We should be starting now in preparation for 5 years from now … we'll always have a cyclical hump. Districts should bank more money to get us through the next fiscal hump. We need to work on a business model."
- "Solely, Solely based on budget….Took all the cuts the first year to then reap the savings for future years. True fiscal pressure of the economy."
- With the passing of Prop 30 there was an acknowledgement that we needed to do it now or else things would be worse. It increased the sense of urgency to make good decisions. We are still in a position financially where we haven't quite right-sized yet."
- "We were living outside of our means for some time."
- "The initial goal from the outset was to reduce the number of programs we offered. We simply had too many."
- "We should have done this before the budget cuts. But we didn't have a process. We have to ask ourselves once in a while, 'what are we doing and why are we doing it?'"

The impact of leadership turnover and acceptable past practices was also mentioned:

- "We had seven deans over the CTE area in eight years. Programs that didn't have fulltime faculty ran the show and faculty had a lot of power as a result. We ran courses that had 25% enrollment, overloaded part-time faculty, offered multiple low-enrolled sections, etcetera. Going through this process was the only way to put an end to some of these crazy practices. Program discontinuance was a healthy reset of the relationship between the college and the programs."

- "The CTE area was sorely neglected due to administrative turnover. Series of courses were created more to secure employment for part time faculty."
- "There were some programs in my mind that needed to be eliminated or worked on and we didn't have the time to spend on revitalization or reinvigorate them, but there were some limping programs that didn't serve community need, and didn't lead to a job or transfer. We knew a few for a long time; so those were easy to make decisions about."

A few comments touched on change management and the need to evaluate programs even when the climate is stable:

- "When we're fat and happy we don't tend to look at those things" [in context of program vitality and program review]
- "In good times, no one was paying that much attention. But we should still be looking at the purpose and role of each program on the front end through ongoing, continuous evaluation; then we wouldn't need to cut things for monetary purposes."

One poignant statement discovered during archival research was this acknowledgement of the difficult PD work from a college president:

- "This is one of the most difficult tasks any organization undertakes— taking a hard, comprehensive look at a program with identified needs, analyzing it carefully, and providing creative recommendations for program improvement and/or potential reduction"

HUMAN RESOURCE FRAME

It seems most appropriate to begin the discussion of the human resource frame with this interview quote from a faculty member: "A college is curriculum and it is people. You can talk about buildings and processes and policies, but what we teach and the people that make it possible is what a college is. And when you're dealing with those two things, it can be sticky."

The overarching convergent pattern identified from multiple institutions researched was the correlation between feeling that one's opinion was heard and their support/buy-in of the final outcome. There were both faculty and administrative personal who commented that they were not consulted formally or informally, and thus they expressed discontent, dissatisfaction, (or in one case) complete ambivalence. One faculty referred to a phenomenon they called "summer magic" when "change happens when everyone is away." It is worth noting that an appropriate balance between the political and human resource frames must be achieved; and this was noted by a number of individuals interviewed. As one senior administrator noted:

> It takes decisive leadership with an understanding of what people are going through. People feel picked on, misunderstood…you have to work through and bring people along to the point they understand it is not about them; it is about institutional survival and getting through a tough time. Doesn't mean they are gone forever—just not effective enough to be maintained under this set of circumstances. As circumstances change, who knows, it could be brought back 10 years from now.

A related aspect of this convergent pattern identified across institutions was the lack of engagement, communication, and/or involvement in PD with part-time faculty. Regardless of full-time faculty representation within an affected CTE area, part-time faculty members were not as engaged in the multiple PD processes researched, while admittedly affected by their outcome. In some instances the administration was very conscious to disseminate communications to all faculty members regardless of discipline or their employment status as fulltime versus part-time. However, few individuals interviewed cited heavy engagement or involvement by part time faculty members. As one employee noted, "We didn't really follow our process; just eliminated programs that did not have fulltime faculty…easy way to cut without doing the hard work." It was also stated that a number of part time faculty did lose the opportunity to continue teaching at institutions where programs were discontinued. The impact of discontinued programs specifically on part-time faculty is an area warranting additional research in the future.

Conversely, others heavily engaged in the process became very threatened in turf battles where resources were perceived as being taken away. This resulted in defensive behavior (which for two institutions still persists years later) within both the faculty and administrative classifications. In multiple instances, these interpersonal battles were attributed to poor, or inconsistent, leadership. One faculty participant observed that their discipline had experienced significant leadership turnover (7 Deans in 8 years) not facilitating any strategic partnership building or program planning within the division.

Due to the snowball sampling method employed in the case study research, I interviewed a few faculty members that were not directly involved in the PD committee work, or decision making process, but were affected by the final outcome. In spite of archival evidence documenting communications and process steps, most felt blindsided by the final decisions and/or the very process itself. Some were completely unaware of the time and resources devoted to reviewing the program in question, and felt that victory was given to the individual that simply screamed the loudest.

A number of individuals during the interviews noted that CTE programs are very reliant upon faculty leadership; thus programs without full-time faculty were significantly at risk of being discontinued. This human factor came into play with CTE programs that had a faculty member retire; especially in single-person departments when their retirement left the academic program without a fulltime faculty champion. In commenting about the impact the PD process had at the college, one interviewee stated, "no one lost their job, but it sped up the process for a few to retire." At multiple institutions researched, a golden handshake and/or retirement incentive occurred around the same time as their PD process which also impacted the decision for some faculty to leave (and arguably to some, thus, some programs to be discontinued). In another instance, faculty transferred from one college to another within the same district to "right-size" the academic offerings while preserving faculty employment in that discipline.

In higher frequency than the other three frames, a number of direct quotes from the interviews were very germane to the Human Resource frame and collectively they help to illustrate the complexities inherent within the PD process and the people involved. Many respondents commented about their feelings as they underwent the PD process.

- "There was a lot of heated exchange and people were pissed off, but it really was a collaborative effort."
- "Most people stay here their entire career; strong in that sense. But strained relationships. We need some healing … there are some hurt feelings. It affected us. It will take a while to get past that cause people are still here."
- One faculty member stated, "Whenever the PD process happens, faculty feel it is happening to them—it is territorial. They'll say, 'They can't tell me what to do with my program.'"
- "It was a horrendous, draining, straining process. Not fun to tell a colleague that you were going to eliminate their program."
- "I feel punished for trying to make my program better. I'm much more bitter now; in a much darker spot. I was looking for another job. Won't take chances now. Won't upgrade or change program again until I die."
- "It was a painful process. Some were empathetic, but my program was deemed not part of the college mission."
- "I was numb when this all hit me."

Many others commented about individuals feeling heard and valued during the process:

- "I would have started with the faculty impacted by each area. But since it had to be done quickly we made the decision by this elite body.…Perhaps even if time an open meeting so that people could speak and give input for things that the [group] should have considered. But, overall people tend to feel better if they were brought in earlier…it was surprising to some. People didn't know that programs were on a list."

- "What was more upsetting is what went unsaid. It felt like a shell of a process with no real understanding."
- "Those that went through it thought they should have been given more time and didn't get a fair shake."

Others commented on serving on the committee which reviewed their peers, and how it felt to make difficult decisions:

- "When you make complex recommendations about how something should evolve and you make that decision, then you have to talk to the people involved, and those people (faculty or staff) have to then implement change; and change is hard."
- "Our process is healthy and amazing but it comes with a cost. If you insist on being involved, be aware there is a cost. You are part of the decision process in getting rid of your peers."
- "The dragging of the feet occurred at the admin level. They had a report with the recommendations, and they had to make tough decisions which were delayed. But I also understand how difficult that is because it all involves personnel. There are all kinds of pieces to it. These are complex decisions."
- "It's scary to go through the first time. It was really, really hard to be a member of that group making a decision on your peers."
- "…it was hard to fight for one small program when people were losing their jobs all around you. Tough to consider the program without the people; a knot in the stomach the whole time."
- "How do you tell your peers that what they've given their life to is no longer valid and that you are redundant?"
- "It's a catch-22 with faculty leadership who want to make things better, but they end up needing to make difficult decisions that might subtract something from an institution… I thought we were all working together. There was a real stop in the process when faculty realized what they were actually doing and the consequences of this were real."
- "How do you tell a colleague that they are not relevant anymore? Need an outside party to come in and do that."

Some commented on the process itself, the way the situation was initially introduced, or how the management of the process significantly mattered:

- One faculty noted that had the entire situation been explained differently from the onset, instead of the budget being a primary driver, that, "it might have gone over a lot differently. It's all about how you approach people."
- Another faculty mentioned that, "If ego can be removed, or at least tried to be removed, and if we are asked, not told, then it works a lot better and we can make this the best place possible."
- "In that meeting, the facilitators need to set up ground rules in advance for how you speak about programs and about each other … what you can or cannot talk about. Your own personal opinions or emotions should not be included; only to discuss what is on the paper."
- "They could have very easily abstained from the vote … we had to keep them from abstaining by helping them understand the value of their work."
- "It was a really unsettling program discontinuance process. Most were aware we had a program and were willing to move forward with the discontinuance process, but were not prepared for the scope of what we needed to look at or the speed by which we needed to move."
- "The programs I saw go through the process all survived because it motivated faculty to be more forward looking."

A few commented on the importance of fulltime status and personal relationships:

- "I am a well-liked person, so it wasn't like they wanted to get rid of me. I am active on campus. Not the same for some others. If not active with a personal relationship….I can say I had a little bit of an advantage."
- "Any program without a fulltime faculty was vulnerable. One interpretation is because it was difficult with part-timers with narrow programs; they may not have been able to do the program review documents to get us ready for accreditation. Program couldn't have the quality oversight needed for accreditation purposes; some were also expensive as a comparison of how many students were being impacted; plus the stipend for a lead faculty member."
- "No full-timers were affected by this, just temporary faculty. [They] rented space and equipment, so they weren't really a family member."

Others commented on trust and collaboration within their campus culture:

- "It takes a lot of trust building over time to have these conversations across campus."
- "We drink funny Kool-Aid here. We all get along."
- "Like a family, we have this history and so we need to deal with the 'now' but also need to be mindful that we need to deal with the same people

tomorrow and in the future. What we do now will affect the future as well."

- "Our skill set to have hard conversations was really low"
- "I didn't know if I was being saved or chopped....So now I don't trust any of them."
- "People felt targeted and non-validated. Didn't have enough collaborative trust built-up ahead of time, to rely on that as a campus."

Employees also commented on fiscal/legal matters from a human resources frame:

- "Yes, we needed to quit spending money on programs that were not working. Easy to think about logically, but not from a human perspective."
- "Tried to avoid faculty layoffs. Not one fulltime faculty is losing their job."
- "There may be some factors that start PD that's outside of our control; other times it's a faculty that needs to join the twenty-first century."

POLITICAL FRAME

The PD processes researched emerged as very political processes fraught with turf battles, negotiations, and interpersonal power plays. Some used the PD process to drive their unrelated agendas (e.g. to gain additional support for their program, secure additional faculty members, be able to offer additional sections in their discipline, etc.). Others were focused on future career advancement and/or self-preservation. For example, one employee commented, "I saw the writing on the wall and didn't want to gain more gray hair; so I backed off ... if you stand up and speak out it can only hurt you. So you have to be smart about that ... the process was very political. I need to save myself."

The colleges in this research sample were very strategic in appointing individuals to serve on an ad-hoc PD committee. One college went so far as to include external members (non-district employees) in an attempt to minimize any potential power struggle and maximize objectivity. These individuals were either researchers from a neighboring institution or a representative from the California workforce system.

Another convergent theme illuminated by this research is that the governance system needs to be respectful of the purview of the academic senate in terms of shared governance; and conversations about PD need to have clear limits and boundaries. Until it is clear where their recommendations end, and where the administrative decision starts, the PD process will always be contentious. In one institution analyzed, the historical role of the academic senate took on more authority then their board policy and state law provided them. More specifically, there was an attempt to place everything under "academic and professional matters" and as a result the roles and responsibilities for each constituency group needed to be clarified. The role of the union (faculty bargaining unit) may also be a variable in the PD process depending on the district's contract language. For example, any layoff of fulltime faculty or course cap negotiations would fall under the union's purview as a working condition issue. The curriculum element of PD belongs to the Academic Senate's purview, but bargaining and working conditions falls within the union's purview. In one institutional process included in this case study, the union successfully negotiated increased course caps as a budget savings strategy to protect/spare the college from even more severe program reductions. But when additional cost-savings negotiations failed, program discontinuance processes were triggered.

Additionally, within the political frame the role of the administration and the President's style of leadership were very influential in the PD process; especially if policy modifications were undertaken. As one manager observed, "We tried to free the hands of faculty to deal with [program review] since their final goal is not to save money or cut budget. That's my job. Theirs is to make the best decision for students." Another senior administrator commented:

> When you get to the point of recommending positions or programs, that's when you hit a log jam and no one wants to make the decision. They want participatory governance, but when you try to make them a part of it, they don't want to do it. I understand the fear people have in doing it. So there is a point I need to step in and make the decision—in the end they are grateful cause it takes the heat off of them.

The important role of the president and senior administration in this process echoes Eaton's research which asserts that the top administrators truly spearhead program discontinuance.[4]

Unfortunately, some college personnel used the curriculum as political pawns during the PD process. This occurred by ether by restricting its revision while being evaluated, cross listing courses (or de-cross listing courses) to change their CTE status, or moving specific classes between departments (often based on their transferability or CTE status based on statewide SAMs codes). In one case a specific class was described as given back to another department as part of the bargaining and compromise that occurred during the PD implementation. In another instance, the department at the Cal State University system that taught a particular class was referenced as justification for where the course should be housed at the community college. The number of programs that fell under a given dean or department was also important to many as an unofficial indicator of influence/power.

Another reemerging theme was the divisive language that was used during the interviews. Even though individuals were a part of the same institution, a majority of participants in this case study used "them" versus "us," and "we" versus "them." For example, one faculty member stated, "They needed to show to ACCJC that they had a plan to fix the fiscal issues," instead of internalizing the shared adoption of institutional issues. Another employee commenting on the institution's adoption of policy stated, "I don't know if they would be able to pull that again. The higher one's position in the organizational chart (in both the administrative and faculty ranks) the more deliberate and divisive the language became. The lower-level administrators and non-leadership faculty expressed more inclusive language as part of the college community in describing their experience within the program discontinuance process.

A number of direct quotes from the interviews were very germane to the political frame and worth contemplating. The most frequent adjectives used to describe an institutions PD process were adversarial such as "battle" and "divorce":

- "A lot of our resource were siphoned off...it was a bitter divorce"
- "I had a target on my back for moving the programs forward."
- "Can only do massive cuts across the board so long before it starts to impact student's being able to complete. Needed to reduce the footprint of the college and stop the bleeding."
- "It felt like a really nasty divorce and we had to fight over the kids."
- "[It] was a battle; transfer versus CTE. We fought over a [X] class. It transfers so they wanted to run it. That was a bargain/compromise that occurred."

Others commented about differences between faculty and administrative roles/perspectives:

- "You can't be pro-faculty or pro-administration. You need to be pro-truth."
- "Philosophically if the [faculty] cut nothing, you blame the administration. The hard way about how we did it is that you, the faculty, are in some measure are to blame for it. Interestingly, if you need someone to blame, it is easier to blame the admin."
- "Need to have very strong and committed executive leadership."
- "[Administration] says there will be no PD process next year beyond program planning"
- "Would need to go back years to have prevented this. Really needed to be focused on accreditation. It wasn't on the radar of faculty. Union was not

allowing the administration to require SLOs, so consequently did nothing about it for years."
- "Faculty didn't take the lead, so they lost their voice."

Employees also commented about various systems and processes:

- "Program discontinuance is a symptom of the inability of our governing system"
- "That [accreditation] self-evaluation ended up being a venting document."
- "It was a fairly rational process. There were a lot of politics. Some industry folks spoke to the President."
- "I didn't feel comfortable changing inaccurate recommendations of the sub-group."
- "At some times you felt the process was in your control, and other times you couldn't do anything about it."
- "Faculty wrote in the program plan that the field was reinventing itself. The things put in [their] program plan were used against [them]. He/she didn't know it and felt betrayed by that."
- "We talked about it for a number of years. Curriculum approvals take a number of years…Years ago worked on program review, but never had a high impetus to get rid of anything."
- "[Program X] didn't get on the list. It was a very political, divergent process. Everyone agreed it wasn't appropriate."
- "We tried very hard to make these decisions based on principle— and for the right reasons. No one wanted to do it, but we had to make budget cuts. I wouldn't say we're a better place for the effort as our students now have less choices, but we survived to teach another day."

One's motivations (silent or overt) were also frequently commented upon:

- "I never figured out their motive, I just assumed it was budget based. Now I have stronger administrative support."
- "In the end, even when we were doing it, there was a political angle; they were making the data say what they wanted."
- "I was told not to convene my Advisory Board during the program discontinuation process. It was not properly motivated."
- "I think [X] went through the small programs first and also those areas of potential duplication."
- "They simply didn't like him and wanted him moved."
- "I presented to the Board knowing what I was saying was an absurdity."
- "The program was deleted because [he] wanted the classroom and increased release time"

Many also commented on the legislature, locally elected Board of Trustees, as well as the impact of the regional accreditation body and our state's political system:

- "The college seems in tune with Sacramento, but they move the target too much and then we do too."
- "Over all it [the process] did work, but we were saved by Prop 30."
- "The legislature pushes completers. But degree completion can be an enemy of CTE certificate programs"
- "There's lemonade in the lemons. The accreditation sanction and fiscal problems produced a gun to our head from the Board. The Board gave a directive and a deadline first. Had we not accelerated the process it would not have worked cause it would have been too slow."
- "There was a strong hammer there to cooperate." [in context of ACCJC and the district's Board directives]
- "The recommendation from ACCJC on fiscal stability gave us clout and a reason to address the programs offered. It helped faculty realize the severity of why we needed to do this."

SYMBOLIC FRAME

Without exception, those interviewed shared that program discontinuance at their college was a difficult process. Each college included in this research had symbolic steps to reinforce their culture, be they open memos from the president to the campus community to embrace their transparent communications and self-reflective culture; or town-hall open forums to discuss a program's viability complete with invitations published in the local newspaper symbolic of their inclusive and community-focused culture.

Within multi-college districts there is another factor to consider during PD, namely the institution's academic focus in relation to other sister-institutions. More than one interviewee commented that certain programs were either discontinued or retained due to its place within the district. Symbolically it seemed to matter if programs were offered at other colleges within the district (positively or negatively) as the offerings were often part of the institutional identity, mission, and historical community ties. For example, one "flagship" program was retained during a PD process regardless of the data collected because of the symbolic identity between the community and the college primarily associated with this program.

The faculty at one college understood that program reduction needed to happen and didn't ask why; but they did ask why a certain program. Many agreed with the overall need, but the individual targeting of programs was unsettling—increasingly so when the communication of the process was not perceived/received. It was symbolically paramount that the faculty and administrative leadership were in sync and had regular meetings to discuss the process. That said, multiple interviewees confirmed (both faculty and administrators) that transparency only goes so far and that some conversations (or true feelings) remain behind closed doors. In one particular instance, a faculty member privately agreed with discontinuing a program but later publicly denounced the decision in symbolic support of their fellow faculty members.

A convergent theme throughout this research was the symbolic importance that a college's history played both upon the broader campus culture as well as the specific PD proceedings. As previously mentioned, for example, the legend/history at one college was that "the college was built in the 60's by a bunch of hippies" and this was perceived to play a significant symbolic role in the collaborative tone and dialog-rich culture at the institution. This history-affected culture also penetrated the PD process which ensured that everyone had a chance to speak and be heard. Symbolically, this researcher found the connection between institutional culture and PD process steps to be strong.

Although less commonly touched upon than the other three frames, a number of direct quotes from the interviews were very germane to the symbolic frame. Some comments illustrate the college's symbolic commitment, real or perceived, to certain practices (e.g. transparency, fairness, and open dialog):

- "There were open forums and discussions for the public to express their ideas."
- "It was unanimously voted by the committee not to discontinue it…not sure if it was there just to show that the committee wasn't rubberstamping programs."
- "Giving input at the final Board meeting was too late. Should have come earlier. We just felt like we didn't have the time."
- "At the Board meeting, it was clear people were there to speak to that item, but they went through everything and didn't move the agenda around to accommodate people there. So it was a few hours into the meeting before they got to public comment. They didn't rearrange the agenda, so it was clear they didn't want to hear the people whose livelihood would be affected."
- "Those that put up the best show got saved."
- "At the Board of Trustee meeting when the motion was made and comments were made, one member made the motion, and the student trustee seconded the motion to cut the programs, because they understood the fiscal problem. Huge symbolic move. Would have hurt students more if we went bankrupt."

A few commented on the college's perceived mission and reputation:

- "The college is renowned for not being CTE friendly. The college mission is overtly transfer-focused."
- "We pruned the tree. Some will argue we pruned too much, but time will tell and we can always bring them back."

Other comments highlighted the symbolic nature of relationships, their district's policy, and that of their governance structures:

- "ACCJC required that the college has a program discontinuance policy. Didn't have one until a few years ago and only had it on the books for accreditation."
- "Per 1725, program vitality is the purview of the Academic Senate. The Academic Senate cannot be tainted by the idea or fact that they might be getting rid of someone's job. That burden must fall on the president and administration. The line of recommendation and final recommendations must be a sharp line. That makes it easier for faculty to do the work they need to do."
- "[X] and I would say there cannot be any sunlight between us."
- "We want to separate program revitalization and program elimination into two different processes."
- "Program elimination is a real barometer of where your campus climate is overall"
- "It is tough to cut unless you get to crisis"
- "We had to choose, either a lot of programs that are not adequately funded, or fewer programs that are adequately funded."

NOTES

1. Bolman, L. & Deal, T. (2008). *Reframing Organizations:* Artistry, Choice and Leadership. San Francisco: Jossey-Bass.

2. Ibid.

3. Hefferlin, J. B. L. (1969). *Dynamics of Academic Reform.* San Francisco, CA: Jossey-Bass.

4. Eaton, J. (1992). Presidents and Curriculum. National Center for Academic Achievement & Transfer, 3(8). American Council on Education.

Chapter Seven

California PD Policy Analysis

The importance of understanding the status of community college program discontinuance policies in California is very apparent given the state's unpredictable funding structure. Moreover, in accordance with California Education Code, Title 5, Section 51022, "College districts are required by current regulation and statute to develop a process for program discontinuance and minimum criteria for the discontinuance of occupational programs."

In the whitepaper, "Program Discontinuance: A Faculty Perspective," the Academic Senate for California Community Colleges outlined issues and criteria to consider in creating a PD process.[1] "The development of a program discontinuance process, should be considered within the context of the college mission statement, and should be linked with the college educational master plan and the department's goals and objectives."[2] The ASCCC has recommended that college districts create a process for program discontinuance that takes into account, 1) negative effects on students, 2) college curriculum balance, 3) educational and budget planning, 4) regional economic and training issues, and 5) collective bargaining issues. However, as this chapter will outline not all community college districts in California have an approved policy for program discontinuance; and among those that have an approved policy, the metrics and processes vary widely.

POLICY ANALYSIS METHODOLOGY

This statewide policy review and analysis was conducted to identify and categorize the current metrics mentioned in approved Board Policies and/or their corresponding Administrative Procedures to better understand the variation and innovation across districts in California. My initial hope was that this information will not only provide a benchmark, but that it may also be helpful for districts still creating such policies, as well as for those districts desiring to modify/enhance existing policies in light of changing industry and community needs, economic uncertainty, and evolving institutional goals/ objectives/missions.

The methodology for this policy analysis was to focus on the state's 72 districts, not the 112 community colleges, to review either Board Policies or Administrative Procedures and not mere guidelines or protocols. Thus, there was the anticipation that there would be instances where a particular college may have robust program discontinuance practices in place, but those policies were not included in this analysis if the district's board policy either did not include the same metrics, and/or if it was not accessible on the district website. This distinction was identified to not only keep the analysis manageable, but also to identify those policies that have been formally adopted via each college/district's shared governance processes. This policy analysis is, of course, merely a snapshot in time. A good-faith effort was made to identify all approved/posted CCC District Board Policies and/or Administrative Procedures related to program discontinuance; however some districts seem to have policies still in development that, since not finalized, were not included herein.

In identifying the existence of a PD Board Policy, or Administrative Procedure, for each college district, the variables to be collected were to include:

1. If each of the 72 community college districts in California have a current Board Policy (BP) or Administrative Procedure (AP) for program discontinuance.
2. The number of colleges within each district.
3. The name/title of the policy.
4. Ant legal references cited in the policy.
5. The length of the policy (page length).
6. Date the policy was approved.
7. The stated reasons/variables to initiate a PD process.
8. The person/group that initiates the PD process.
9. Those cited as participating in the PD process.
10. Stated time allowed before the process must conclude.
11. The variables/data considered in determining if a given CTE program should be maintained, revised, or discontinued.
12. Any additional policy considerations stated if a program is discontinued (e.g. faculty reassignment, students in the pipeline).

The result of this thorough document analysis of the 72 CCC district policies for program discontinuance was summarized in a database notating the above 12 variables/factors as well as a narrative analysis of any commonalities and outliers (currently posted on the CCCCO website at this time of this printing). This policy analysis will result in a better understanding of the structural and procedural conditions within which program discontinuance can occur.

POLICY INVENTORY AND ANALYSIS RESULTS

Among the 72 community college districts in California, program discontinuance policies and/or administrative procedures were identified for sixty districts. No policy was found for twelve districts. Out of the sixty policies/ procedures identified, fifty-eight can be located online at district or college websites; and two were found via personal communications. Each policy document identified was then reviewed and analyzed for a set of specific criteria following the methodology initially outlined. The raw results of this review are summarized in the policy inventory spreadsheet posted on the CCCCO website. This policy inventory spreadsheet includes each policy's or procedure's number, title, internet hyperlink, length in number of pages, date approved or last modified, the stated initiators of the program discontinuance process, metrics used to trigger/initiate a program discontinuance process, mention of the committee membership, stated metrics/variables used during the program discontinuance process to evaluate a program and determine next steps, the process duration, stated possible outcomes of the review, additional policy considerations stated, and references cited. If the policy was silent on a particular item, the cell was left blank. What follows are some descriptive statistics and frequencies highlighting the key findings.

Policy Title, Length, and Date

Titles of the policies and procedures related to program discontinuance vary from district to district. The most common title used was "Program Discontinuance". Thirty-five districts used this title to describe their policies, with some variation in language (e.g. "discontinuance process," "academic program discontinuance," etc.). Eight out of the sixty districts (13%) included program discontinuance/revitalization provisions within a broader policy or procedure focused on program/curriculum development, review, and modification. Common policy titles in these cases were "Program and Curriculum Development" and "Program Management." Three of the districts have only developed discontinuance policies for career and technical/occupational programs; hence, the titles of their policies were specific to CTE. Other titles utilized by the community college districts included the following: "Program Viability," "Program Modification," "Program Vitality," "Program Revitalization," "Program Appraisal and Recommendation Process."

Among the policies reviewed, 57 provided the date(s) when the current language of the procedure/process was approved and/or revised. Many of these policies are very recent. Fifteen districts (26%) approved or revised them since 2011–2012. Twenty-three policy documents (40%) can be considered "fairly recent" as they were developed/modified from 2008-2010. The remaining 19 policies (33%) were approved or modified between 2000 and 2007.

In terms of the length of the policy text, the program discontinuance policies reviewed ranged from 1 to 16 pages in length. Many documents (12 out of 60) were relatively short totaling one page or less. Without exception, these shorter policies were not very specific and provided only general guidelines related to program discontinuance approaches, without stating any evaluation criteria, process timeline and considerations, or other related details The majority of policies, however, were 2–6 pages in length providing additional process instruction and detail. Only a few documents reviewed exceeded seven pages of content.

Initiation and Committee Membership

Only 43 out of the 60 districts with policies and/or procedures provided language related to the initiation of the program discontinuance process. The guidelines range from "any member of the college community" who could trigger the process to a specified list of individuals or departments/committees who are entitled to do so. While the districts differ in terms of who can initiate the program discontinuance process, most policies agree that either Vice President of Academic Affairs, Vice President of Instruction, Vice President of Student Services, Dean of the affected program (or program manager/director/coordinator), or faculty of the affected program (or Academic Senate representative) are in a position to recommend a program for discontinuance or revitalization review. Other members of college community who may trigger the process in some districts include: Department/Division Chair, Curriculum Committee Chair, Education Planning Committee Chair, Advisory Committee Chair, Program Review Chair, Articulation Officer, Students, or the Governing Board. Interestingly, only seven of the 60 policies tie the beginning of the program discontinuance process to the program review results and not to an individual. Conversely, there are also a few policies that differentiate between program review and program discontinuance as two separate and distinct processes serving two different purposes that should not be connected.

Most community college districts prescribe the establishment of a task force or an ad hoc committee to lead the evaluation of a program recommended for discontinuance. Forty-seven of the districts provide guidelines regarding the membership of such a task force or committee. In a few cases, these guidelines are rather general requiring the district to include "all parties potentially affected by the decision (faculty, staff, administrators, students, the employing businesses and industries, and the community)." Most districts, however, outline the membership of a committee in more detail. The most common members of a program discontinuance task force/committee that appear in the majority of reviewed policies are:

- Faculty from the affected program
- Division dean or other administrator(s)
- Other faculty representatives (usually appointed by the Academic Senate)
- Vice President of Instruction or other senior level administrator(s)

Other members that are mentioned by about 20–30% of policies include:

- Department chair(s)
- Counselor(s)
- Student(s)
- Classified staff representative(s)
- Institutional research
- Academic Senate president or designee
- Curriculum committee chair or representative(s)
- Dean outside of the affected program area

More rarely, the following interest groups and/or individuals are included in the discussions:

- Advisory committee member (only 6 out of 60 policies prescribes representation from an advisory board)
- Local workforce investment boards (in consultation capacity)
- Program review committee chair or representative
- Community
- College President

Initiation Variables/Metrics Cited

Program discontinuance policies and procedures were reviewed for the criteria that are used by the districts to initiate the process. Among the policies identified, 37 provided specific metrics or general guidelines regarding what variables may or may not be used for such purposes. Most commonly cited metrics are changing/decreasing labor market demand and low/declining enrollment (23 districts, 38%, state these variables), followed by the program review and analysis of trends (16 districts; 27%). Other common criteria include the availability of human, physical, or fiscal resources; low student completion; low retention or persistence; transfer trends, etc. Notably, some districts (10 of the 60) specifically state in their policies and/or procedures that budgetary considerations should not be used to initiate program discontinuance discussions. Conversely, other institutions include such variables as budget reductions, program cost, and availability of facilities and other resources among their criteria for process initiation.

Program Discontinuance Process Variables/Metrics Cited

While some program discontinuance policies provide only broad guidelines about the discussion process, many also outline the variables that may (or must) be considered to assess whether a program should to be revitalized, discontinued or continued without change. Forty-two out of the 60 policies analyzed were found to include such lists. The evaluation metrics included in the policies can be categorized into two groups: qualitative and quantitative. In fact, certain districts have organized their recommended variables this way in the printed policy. Many policies emphasize the importance of evaluating qualitative aspects of a given program instead of solely focusing on quantitative metrics.

Among the most frequently used qualitative metrics for assessing program viability are: 1) regional duplication or replication, i.e. the existence of a similar program at other local colleges (28 policies contain this variable; 47% of all policies identified), 2) impact of program discontinuance on other programs or cross discipline projects within the college (27; 45%), and 3) match of the program with the college mission, educational master plan, goals and objectives (22; 37%). Other common qualitative criteria include effect on students, potential for disproportionate impact on diversity, balance of college curriculum, community need, ability of students to complete their educational goals using the program, and the quality of the program as perceived by such groups as students, businesses, and community. Many of the variables cited were also recommended in the Academic Senate document. Interestingly, program advisory committee recommendations and employer satisfaction are the metrics that appear in the district policies less frequently; only 15 and 9 policies cite these variables, respectfully.

The majority of policies reviewed cited the following quantitative assessment variables: labor market trends, including current and projected employment and industry wages (38 of the 60 policies, 63%, included this variable); low and/or declining student enrollment for a significant period of time (35 policies; 58%); and program completion/achievement rates (33; 55%). Other frequently cited quantitative metrics are retention and persistence rates, frequency of course section offerings and scheduling trends, employment placement rates, efficiency and productivity of enrollment, FTES generated, resources available, etc. Similarly to the initiation criteria, budgetary concerns are included in the program viability discussions by only a few community college districts. Primary attention is given to the student enrollment, persistence, and completion as well as demand for the program in the region.

Process Duration

From among those policies reviewed, only 24 of 60 clearly state how long the program discontinuance discussions should take place before a final decision is made. Those that do provide such guidance vary greatly on the recommended duration. Specifically, the following durations are cited: 1 semester or less (8 policies), from 2 semesters to 2 years (12 policies), over 2 years (4 policies).

Stated Possible Outcomes

Most district policies (44 out of 60) define possible outcomes of the program discontinuance discussions. The majority of policies state that the committee deliberations should result in one of the following three outcomes:

- *Recommendation to Continue or Accept the Program in its Current State.* A program is recommended to continue without any changes when it has been determined that it is in the best interest of the college, students, and the larger community to do so.
- *Recommendation to Continue with Qualifications/Modifications (Revitalization Plan).* A program is recommended to continue with qualifications when it has been determined that interventions are necessary in order to strengthen the program and/or improve its viability and responsiveness. Consistently, policies state that such a decision should be accompanied by a specific plan of actions and agreed upon timeline to revitalize the program. Most policies include provisions specifying that the program affected is to be reviewed again upon the completion of the revitalization plan and schedule. Some districts' policies also incorporate specific revitalization strategies for each of the possible problem areas, thus providing more detailed guidance to a program discontinuance committee/task force (e.g. Mira Costa Community College District).
- *Recommendation to Discontinue.* A program is declared obsolete and recommended for discontinuance when it has been concluded that it is no longer viable (i.e. it falls outside the district/college's mission, strategic goals, and/or the department's goals and objectives). The majority of the policies stipulate only permanent discontinuance of a program. However, as an exception, Pasadena Community College District's policy indicates that a program may be "discontinued permanently" or "discontinued with the curriculum placed in inactive status," and after three years of inactive

status, a program is automatically dropped from the District's inventory of programs. This particular decision rule seems to support the contentious claim that programs advertised in catalogs are not offered.

Although less common, additional outcomes stated by individual community college district policies include: Program consolidation (consolidation of class sections from two or more colleges at one college in order to preserve the program or major), an additional review of the program (when consensus is not reached), program extension or suspension, departmental reorganization, program initiation, or program reduction.

References Cited

A number of policies cited specific institutional documents or additional Education Code sections. A large majority of policies cited at least the following four references:

- Education Code Section 78016, Review of program: Termination
- Title 5 Section 51022, Program Discontinuance
- Title 5 Section 55130, Approval of Credit Programs
- Program Discontinuance: A Faculty Perspective. ASCCC, adopted Spring 1998

Discontinuance Considerations

When a program is recommended for discontinuance, most policies state additional provisions that need to be considered by the college in their program discontinuation plan. Most widely cited provision is the consideration for the students who are currently enrolled in the affected program. The majority of policies (42 of 60) state that enrolled students should be allowed to complete their programs of study and their catalog rights must be maintained and accounted for in allowing them to finish the program in question. Secondly, maintaining collective bargaining commitments and reassigning and/or retraining program faculty are the other common policy considerations found in the program discontinuance policies. Many policies clearly state that discontinuance plans need to incorporate the implementation of all requirements of collective bargaining for faculty and staff, including the application of policies for reduction in force.

Other provisions cited, albeit less frequently, include updating the program inventory with the California Community College Chancellor's Office, removing the discontinued program from the catalog, assessing impact on budget and facilities, and/or considering any articulation agreements currently in place.

SUMMARY POLICY OBSERVATIONS

While the primary methodology of this policy analysis was simply to categorize the elements present in existing policies, there are some notable observations worth mentioning. Overall, comprehensive policies seemed to incorporate the following components: 1) metrics to determine if a program should be evaluated/considered for discontinuance, 2) the workflow, process steps, and appropriate timeline, 3) Encouraging both quantitative and qualitative metrics used to evaluate if a program should be retained, modified, or discontinued.

We know that economic factors and budgetary constrains greatly impact the development or discontinuance of academic programs. However, some policies specifically expressed that the institution's budget and economic constraints should not be considered as part of a given program's evaluation (e.g. Glendale CCD). Other policies specified the specific fiscal considerations and formulas to use in determining if the revenue received and resources available were adequate to maintain the program in question (e.g. San Luis Obispo CCD).

There were additional factors beyond just the budget that were inconsistent across district policies in California. For example, some districts combine the Program Review forms/process with the Program Discontinuance forms/data/process (e.g. Contra Costa CCD), while other district policies make a point that the processes are to remain distinctively separate (e.g. Redwoods CCD). In a third category, multiple districts cite that program review data may be considered during evaluating a program for discontinuance, but that the processes are still separate. Moreover, only 22 district policies specifically included the "Employability and Employment Placement Rate" as a metric to evaluate within a program vitality or discontinuance process. In light of the research literature and the recent federal mandate of gainful employment disclosure requirements, perhaps the inclusion of this metric should be revisited by community college districts.

In another example, only those policies approved/modified within the last few years included the assessment of student learning outcomes, or program learning outcomes, as a variable to consider in evaluating for program discontinuance. Noting its exclusion may be an opportunity for districts to revise existing policies. And finally, only a small minority of policies specified receiving feedback from their local Industry Advisory Board, and/or the Workforce Investment Board as part of the program vitality or discontinuance process. These were the main areas of inconsistency that districts should pay particular attention to in revising these policies in the future.

A number of policies in California had unique elements included that made them stand out from the others. Some specific examples include:

- Hartnell CCD and Cabrillo CCD's policy differentiated between the quantitative metrics to evaluate for CTE programs versus the quantitative metrics to evaluate for Transfer programs.
- Chabot-Las Positas' policy and Gavilan's policy both specifically require three metrics to be met in order to trigger/initiate a program discontinuance process.
- The duration of the process varies greatly from one single term (e.g. Chaffey CCD) to 2-4 years (e.g. Riverside CCD).
- A few policies included appendices with helpful templates/resources. West Hills CCD's policy includes an "Occupational Program Two-Year Review form" and Sonoma County CCD's policy includes question prompts for a self-evaluation report.
- In addition to Program Modification, Improvement, or Discontinuance, Los Angeles CCD lists two other potential outcomes: Program Initiation, and Departmental Reorganization.
- Golden West College has a detailed process for instructional programs, and a second for student services programs, including timelines and process steps.
- A few district policies (such as Marin CCD and Shasta-Tehama-Trinity Joint CCD) provide a provision to forego the lengthy evaluation process if the discipline faculty voluntarily submits a request to discontinue a program.
- Some multi-college districts outline the metrics/data that colleges should take into consideration (e.g. Ventura County CCD), while other multi-college districts leave it entirely up to each college to decide (e.g. South Orange County CCD).
- Most districts seem to leave it up to the program discontinuance task force/evaluation committee to decide what action can be applied to revitalize a program. However, a small number of districts actually provide a list of possible strategies for each potential situation (e.g. Mira Costa CCD).

NOTES

1. Academic Senate for California Community Colleges (Spring, 1998). *Program Discontinuance: A Faculty Perspective.*
   2. Ibid, p. 9.

Chapter Eight

Answers to Key Research Questions

As more fully explained in the appendix, my first main research question was: Under what conditions does CTE program discontinuance occur? The 3 related sub-questions this research aimed to answer included: 1) How did the process occur?, 2) How did people feel about the process?, and 3) Are actual programs offered aligned with those published? Given previous research completed on program accretion, organizational change, and bureaucratic inertia, program discontinuance seems to be at odds with the very nature/culture of higher education institutions; yet programs do in fact get deleted. This research's hypothesis was that PD would be a rational process, rooted in metric evaluation, resulting from external pressure and fiscal constraint. As a result of this research, it was discovered that CTE program discontinuance in fact most commonly occurs 1) when fiscal resources are reduced externally, 2) when a key administrative catalyst triggers a PD process, 3) when there is no full-time faculty to champion and provide leadership to the CTE program, and/or 4) when the college has an annual program review cycle that measures program vitality in a comprehensive manner. Moreover, Hefferlin's theory of academic reform states that the reform of existing academic curriculum most often occurs during times of instability and vulnerability.[1] This research strongly validates this claim as evidenced by the recent fiscal instability within the California's Community College system.

Regarding the sub-question, "How did the process occur?," only 43 out of the 60 districts with board approved policies provided language related to the initiation of the program discontinuance process. This research revealed that it was key individuals (whom were both able and willing to engage local politics and academic reorganization) who were necessary in triggering a PD process. Without exception, the key individual was an academic administrator regardless of the specific policy language. This research also indicated that the campus culture was not a direct catalyst affecting whether or not a program discontinuation process began, but interviewees confirmed that culture definitely impacted the smoothness and transparency of the process as well as the frequency of communication and policy implementation. In one instance, the PD process impacted the institutional culture in the short-term, and not vice versa. Data from the case studies and archival review helped to illuminate the role of culture on program discontinuance, although a definitive resolution would require investigation beyond the scope of this research. Interestingly, only seven of the 60 policies analyzed connected the beginning of the program discontinuance process to the program review results; but those that did so expressed in the interviews that this connection was extremely beneficial and fostered transparency.

Taking into account Birnbaum's theory of procedural justice[2] and Bolman and Deal's human resource frame,[3] this research study aimed to identify the feelings, experiences, perceptions, and reactions of those directly involved in order to answer the second sub-question: How did people feel about the process? The case study interviews made it very apparent that both the faculty members and administrators leading the program discontinuation efforts felt that the right decisions were ultimately made that, albeit painful at times, greatly benefited the institution in the long term. For institutions that achieved role clarity among constituency groups, their expressed comfort with the process was verbalized as more positive. However some of the individually affected faculty members, especially part-time faculty, often did not understand the process steps or reasons for merging and/or discontinuing academic programs which created long-standing resentment and distrust. Moreover, CTE programs taught only by part-time faculty members, absent fulltime faculty leadership and advocacy, were more prone to program discontinuance.

My last question, "Are actual programs offered aligned with those published?" was included in this text because some community colleges do not offer all the programs that are listed in their catalog or advertised in the state inventory.[4] Thus I analyzed the actual program offerings versus those advertised and published and found that actual programs offered aligned with those published, or there was a one-year lag due to catalog printing deadlines. As mentioned prior, a best practice exhibited by one of the colleges included in this study was to communicate multiple times in various ways (e-mail, in class, and postal mail) to affected students alerting them to the academic program modification/discontinuance and all their possible options for completing their program of study. It is recommended that colleges looking to discontinue CTE programs put forth the extra effort to identify and analyze the students in the affected program and to ensure the completion of their program of study is not thwarted.

The second main research question for this study was: What is the role of policy in program discontinuance? This research inquired about the structural and symbolic involvement of PD policy within successful PD practices, and discovered that most community colleges do have a PD policy (60 were identified among California's 72 districts), and those included in this case study sample remained true to their PD policy (even including one case of a temporarily modified policy). In summary, this research identified that the structure of one's PD policy, especially the ad hoc committee structure and metrics evaluated throughout the procedures, are extremely pivotal in ensuring the accurate and appropriate vitality review of CTE programs.

The process and implementation of program discontinuance is ultimately one type of organizational change and thus in addition to organizational development theory, change management theory is also at play within these situations. As one research participant stated at the conclusion of their interview:

> I just feel that this is a snapshot of transition and evolution and sometimes that's never smooth or easy or ideal…it's sticky and contentious and it is called discontinuance for a reason. It is going to have complexities. It is not about the honeymoon period but the arguments and all the other things. I think that is important to note…Faculty in leadership, administration, and everyone else has learned, but change is messy. Colleges need to change in order to be relevant, so it will often be messy.

As a result of this study which focused upon this alleged "messy" process of program discontinuance, a number of areas relevant for practice in the field emerged. While there were many additional insights and implementation suggestions embedded in the previous chapters, the following chapter outlines eleven specific observations/recommendations for PD process and policy considerations for educators in the field.

NOTES

1. Hefferlin, J. B. L. (1969). *Dynamics of Academic Reform*. San Francisco, CA: Jossey-Bass.

2. Birnbaum, R. (1989). *How Colleges Work: The Cybernetics of Academic Organization and Leadership*. San Francisco, CA: Jossey-Bass Publishers.

3. Bolman, L. & Deal, T. (1997). *Reframing Organizations*. San Francisco: Jossey-Bass. And: Bolman, L. & Deal, T. (2008). *Reframing Organizations:* Artistry, Choice and Leadership. San Francisco: Jossey-Bass.

4. Shulock, N., Moore, C., and Offenstein, J. (2011). *The Road Less Traveled: Realizing the Potential of Career Technical Education in the California Community Colleges*. Sacramento, CA: Institute for Higher Education Leadership & Policy.

Chapter Nine

Next Steps

Eleven Implications for Practice and Policy

Generally speaking, any long-term, sustaining, and substantive changes will occur in public education only if implemented at the grassroots level—in local communities and institutions.[1] In short, the "silver bullet" answer to creating and sustaining relevant Career & Technical Education programs may not come from legislators in Sacramento; it must be engineered and cultivated one person, and one college, at a time. This case study research helped to identify a number of avenues for this change process to occur, eleven of which are discussed below to assist with those engaged in a program discontinuance process in the future.

First, the duration of a given PD process should not span more than one year. Those interviewed for this research indicated that a process 2-years in length (or longer) causes too much strain and affected relationships negatively. In some cases, the process was elongated due to temporary vacancies/interims in key administrative positions, waiting for more data, or other institutional priorities requiring everyone's focus (e.g. accreditation). Regardless, increased pain and havoc was identified in this research by not abiding by strict and efficient timelines in regard to the district's approved PD policy/process. One manager interviewed suggested that the college should "identify one manager to take the arrows, do it fast, and then work to get over it." Another faculty member stated, "It is important to get faculty through the process in under a year otherwise it demoralizes them." A third stated, "we shortened the timeline so that feedback occurred to happen all in the fall to be finished by early spring…the time lag was too long the first year so we shortened it up and make it public as soon as possible." And yet another quipped, "The policy is not functional as written. It is not going to accomplish the stated goal. It is not sufficient for crisis mode operation; need a crisis mode or expedited process that can be enacted."

From among the board policies analyzed, only 24 of 60 clearly state how long the program discontinuance discussions should take place before a final decision is made (and only four policies documented a process longer than two years). Too short of a process (e.g. two months) may be perceived as too quick a process not allowing all constituency groups time to communicate, plan for student teach outs, and solicit community feedback. From the state-wide policy analysis, one academic year is the average timeline to properly process a PD cycle. Also, if a college experiences any timeline delays, that fact also needs to be clearly communicated. As one interviewee articulated, "It is only fair that if you say you're going to make a decision by June, then you need to make it by June and be clear about what that entails; and if you can't with all of its details, then you need to be clear about that as well."

Secondly, over time personnel may shift and individuals may forget the decisions made months or years ago. Colleges should implement specific strategies that both foster and document transparent dialog. One best practice that emerged from this research was to not only have minutes from meetings, but to document the committee's recommendation and have every member in attendance provide a signature in affirmation and attach that to the minutes for future archival reference. Those not in agreement would be noted with a reason documented. This provided one college with transparent, collaborative documentation to prevent the future perception of the decision being manipulated or controlled by any one individual (be it administration or faculty members). This also created a record to share with part-time faculty that may not have been able to fully engage in the process. A separate college videotaped the open forums which discussed programs being reviewed for discontinuance. These videos were posted on the college website for transparency and so that everyone had access. During subsequent conversations, if someone started a distrusting dialog, one could point to that website and encourage the interested party to collect the facts for themselves. A best practice is to identify a group of faculty to work with administration in the review of every number in every PD report to learn and validate the numbers reported. From one college, this practice instills "much more confidence, much less fear and a sense that we are on the right track." Regardless of the specific tactics used, colleges should be cognizant of the aforementioned procedural justice theory[2] and adopt practices that both foster and document transparent dialog.

Third, successful community colleges navigating program discontinuance had very clear communication regarding the process steps. As outlined in the statewide policy analysis, district policies should document the purpose of a PD process, the definition of a program, the metrics and indicators included in the program's evaluation, and a very clear numerated/outlined process which includes the title and role of specific individuals, process steps, milestones of communication, timelines, and definitive deliverables/resolutions. Moreover, more faculty than not were unaware of their institutional policy for PD. Although there was a frequent verbalization for transparency throughout the process, one recommendation that emerged is to ensure all affected faculty (including all recently hired part-time instructors) and administrators are forwarded the official Board Policy and/or procedures/timelines. As stated by one interviewee, "something I would do differently is be sure of really good communications during the process so that there is no idea that a group of people are in a room secretly making decisions…Communicate delays and steps in the process." Doing so will (hopefully) increase everyone's awareness of the institutional process with potential increases in participation and/or understanding. In e-mails, letters, as well as in PD related meetings, repeating the policy and its intentions would also help reinforce the connection (both real and perceived) between PD policy and practice.

Fourth, many PD policies should document additional possible outcomes as a result of undertaking a PD process. In this research, a number of CTE programs were retained, but appropriately modified. For a few programs, segmenting the market and identifying a core target population for the program (e.g. daytime students, versus nighttime, versus online, versus Saturdays) made the difference between program reduction as opposed to discontinuance. During a robust PD process, colleges should consider the frequency of offerings and the target population(s) the program's current composition serves. A district's PD policy should recommend, if not require, such a market analysis and student segmentation to explore the viability of a program modification. Thus, as identified through the state policy analysis, possible outcomes stated within individual community college district policies should include the following options: continuation of program in its current state, program revitalization, program modification, program reduction/refocusing to specific market segments, program consolidation/merging/reorganization, additional review/extension, or program discontinuance.

Fifth, in the spirit of the structural frame, successful PD processes seem to follow a particular process-flow in identifying the programs that should be discontinued: a) identify the metrics that will be compiled and evaluated, often via approved policy; b) either internally (loosely coupled with the program review process) or externally with the help of a consultant, compile the metrics into a dashboard or scorecard to identify each program's performance; c) a subsequent in-depth evaluation of the program(s) by a representative ad hoc committee which includes qualitative and community impact to evaluate the program's vitality; d) planning and implementation of discontinuance/merging/reduction. However, as one interviewee commented, the PD process is never "done done," but should always be tweaked and adjusted.

Another stated, "The formality of discontinuing a program keeps evolving; there will always be blimps and pains in the first year or two." Thus, institutions may want to anticipate and plan for process assessments and refinements after experiencing the first complete PD cycle.

Sixth, colleges should strongly consider including program discontinuance metrics into the annual program review process enabling the program review evaluation to serve as a loosely-coupled catalyst for a distinctly separate PD evaluative process. A repeated theme during the case studies was the very nature of the catalyst for beginning a given PD process. For many colleges, program review has seemingly transformed into nothing more than a resource allocation process instead of its initial intent which includes goal setting, planning, and evaluation for the improvement of student learning. One interviewee identified that, "the program review process doesn't go anywhere right now; goes to the dean and stops. We need to look at the resources they need to remain viable and either tie-in and link a program that is hurting to the resource allocation processes or review it for discontinuance." Although only seven of the 60 policies included in the statewide policy analysis specifically mentioned coupling the program review results to the program discontinuance process, this research indicates this is a natural and beneficial relationship. A best practice utilized within multiple colleges throughout the state is to include program vitality and discontinuance metrics into the program review process and to connect the program review evaluation as a trigger for a distinctly separate PD evaluative process. This one procedural modification could help significantly connect the college's program review, assessment/evaluation, and program discontinuance efforts.

Seventh, CTE faculty members and academic administrators need to vigilantly get involved with the development of reporting templates and metrics surrounding program discontinuance. Through the policy analysis and the case study interviews, this researcher found that a college's quantitative analysis and metrics may not capture the workforce development needs of a local region. Most faculty and administrators do not understand the role and structure of CTE programs, and some institutional practices (e.g. financial aid encouraging all students to select a terminal AS degree as their educational goal) work against CTE programs. So, a strong education component is needed as well as different CTE metrics for accountability. Budget availability and program costs should not be discarded, but need to be properly evaluated. A particular high-quality CTE program may prepare students for high-wage, high-skill, in-demand jobs, but their completion numbers may be low (indicating the certificate completion count may be too high and students are securing employment prior to completion) and/or their other metrics around effectiveness/efficiency may make a program look bad in comparison to others, such as a high program operational cost. College committees need to be educated that CTE programs throughout the state often have a lower efficiency calculation and that this is not only normal and acceptable, but strategically designed as such.

Because of this, occasionally PD decisions for CTE programs are made using a transfer mindset and transfer metrics (typically a result of a transfer-mission oriented culture). In at least one instance, no CTE representation was involved on the ad hoc committee evaluating CTE program vitality. In another instance, a lack of administrative understanding about the difference between a course versus a program resulted in a single-course EMT program being discontinued since it was considered a stand-alone offering as opposed to a viable program (albeit a short one). In the field, this needs to be properly evaluated. When proper employment data were captured at the local college level, CTE programs with "needs improvement" metrics were able to be retained and supported. When program costs were balanced with labor market need and comparative costs of local proprietary institutions, high-cost programs were retained instead of being perceived as a drain with a low return-on-investment. This research highlights the needs for data to be presented carefully and viewed holistically. This includes ensuring that employment placement rates and advisory board input is captured either during the annual program review data or within the PD evaluation criteria. Individual CTE programs also need a comprehensive plan to track their student's employment and wage gain related to course/program completion.

Eighth, the program discontinuance process can be a very politically charged process, and organizational charts (where programs are housed) do matter. As a practitioner, do not underestimate the impact decisions such as merging departments/programs can have. Even the number and composition of CTE programs within a particular dean or department may be an issue, and/or similar academic disciplines might have different administrative support needs. It is recommended to have clear definitions in place as to what programs fall within a particular division or under a specific dean's leadership, and why. As many academic areas are increasingly interdisciplinary, questions did arise in this research about the proper placement of particular programs within the organizational chart. To quote one interviewee from this research, be very aware of this "sticky issue." Establishing clear institutional definitions and delineating roles prior to starting the PD process is recommended. Additionally, if creating a budget reduction plan to address ongoing structural and operational costs, consider program discontinuance and/or budget reductions equally for the academic and non-academic budgets to remain in compliance with California's 50% law.

Ninth, all program discontinue policies need a clear definition of what the college will deem a program. For some institutions included in this research, anything that leads to a unique body of knowledge was considered a program. Other colleges used the official ACCJC definition, and yet others still used the CA Chancellor's Office designation of a state-approved certificate or degree, ignoring mini certificates under 18 units or certificates of achieve-ment. Practitioners are cautioned to wisely differentiate between programs, disciplines, departments, units, offices, initiatives, clubs, teams, courses, and services. Colleges should discuss what entities should complete annual pro-gram review cycles, as well as which are appropriately susceptible to the district's program discontinuance processes.

Tenth, the specific analytical metrics mentioned in approved program discontinuance policies should be revisited. Only 22 district policies in the state specifically included the "Employability and Employment Placement Rate" as a metric to evaluate within a program discontinuance process. Moreover, only a small minority of policies specified receiving feedback from their local Industry Advisory Board, and/or the Workforce Investment Board as part of the program discontinuance process. In fact, advisory com-mittee recommendations and employer satisfaction are the metrics that ap-pear in the district policies least frequently; only 15 and 9 policies cite these variables, respectfully. These metrics should be discussed for inclusion with-in revised board policies. Additionally, the statewide policy analysis herein revealed a number of provisions that although infrequently cited would be beneficial to include in revised policies, including: Updating the program inventory with the California Community College Chancellor's Office, re-moving the discontinued program from the official college catalog, and as-sessing CTE program impact on budget and facilities. In general, the PD policy questions outlined later should also be reviewed and discussed to assist a given community college district in ensuring its PD policy and corre-sponding administrative procedures adequately serve its local community.

The eleventh and most important recommendation is to remember the students who are served by CTE programs. Practitioners must ensure any course reduction or program discontinuance plan takes into account the stu-dents already in that program of study. Fortunately the majority of policies reviewed in the statewide policy analysis (42 of 60) mentioned that enrolled students should be allowed to complete their programs of study and their catalog rights must be maintained and accounted for in allowing them to finish the program in question. When asked what they would do differently if given the chance, one interviewee cited they would draft individual student letters in alignment with their educational plan indicating the specific classes they would still need to take and when it would be offered. This was com-monly referred to as a "teach out" plan. One institution identified students 50% complete with their program and provided them (via certified mail) a customized future schedule to ensure they knew how to finish their program of study. Another institution partnered with neighboring colleges and shared with students those anticipated course offerings to provide a plethora of scheduling options for students to assist them in completing. Recall that the Accrediting Commission for Community and Junior Colleges (ACCJC) are influential in helping to ensure colleges maintain operating practices that support student learning via the previously mentioned standard: II.A.6.b.

RECOMMENDED POLICY INQUIRY QUESTIONS

The policy analysis informed the larger context of this research and will assist others in understanding the structural and procedural conditions within which program discontinuance can occur. Without knowing additional details specific to each campus, I cannot judge or evaluate specific district policies. Thus, no specific recommendations are included for specific college districts regarding their approved policies (although significant best practices were previously mentioned). This research did, however, generate the following questions to support a college inquiry of its current policy. Answering the following questions can assist a given community college district in ensuring its PD board policy and the corresponding administrative procedures are up-to-date and adequately serve its local community:

- Has your policy been created/reviewed/modified in the last 5 years?
- Does your policy outline an existing process or objective metrics to determine if a program should be evaluated or considered for a program discontinuance process?
- Can multiple stakeholders within the institution initiate a program discontinuance process in your district?
- Is the membership of a program discontinuance committee/task force clearly defined in your written policy?
- Does your board policy include a robust mix of quantitative and qualitative metrics for review during a program discontinuance process to ensure a fair and comprehensive evaluation?
- Given our current and foreseeable economic climate, do those stated metrics include economic factors (e.g. both program cost and program revenue)?
- Does your policy include some of the most frequently cited metrics throughout the state in other district policies including labor market trends, low/declining enrollment, completion, retention, and persistence rates, regional duplication, and impact on other programs and/or cross-discipline projects?
- Does your district policy include additional considerations such as the impact on facilities, articulation agreements, 2+2 Tech Prep pathways, ensuring students with catalog rights can continue progress towards their educational goal, the retraining/reassignment of faculty, and the removal of a program from your catalog as well as the CCCCO Program Inventory?

- Does your policy allow a fair opportunity for discourse and review, but also an expedient timeline to permit the institution to respond rapidly to changing workforce and community needs?
- Does your policy allow for multiple resolutions including program stabilization, restructuring, revitalization, suspension, or discontinuance?

NOTES

1. Lynch, R. L. (1996). In search of vocational and technical teacher education. *Journal of Vocational Education Research, 13*(1).

2. Birnbaum, R. (2004). "The End of Shared Governance: Looking Ahead or Looking Back." In Tierney W., Lechuga, V. (Fall. 2004). *Restructuring Shared Governance in Higher Education*, New Directions in Higher Education, #127, Jossey Bass. p. 5–22.

Chapter Ten

Limitations & Recommendations for Future Research

As with any research project, there are limitations inherent in this research study. Even though a multiple case study research design affords more generalizability that a single-case study, only three selected community colleges in California, each with their unique cultures and processes, were part of this research. As such, any generalizations, assumptions, or transferability of findings to other colleges must be done carefully, if at all. Different findings may emerge from other community colleges depending on size and scope, available resources and organizational structure, policy and administrative procedures in place, campus leadership, and unique college culture.

This study intentionally looked only at community colleges that have successfully completed multiple cycles of CTE program discontinuance. The specific number of programs reviewed, how recent were their deliberations, nor composition of board policy at the time were considered for inclusion in this study. Thus, there may be additional community colleges with successful and effective program discontinuance experience that were not included in this study.

The program discontinuance policy analysis was conducted as a snapshot in time even though district board policies are routinely changing. The researcher presumes that some district policies may have been adopted or modified in-between the initial policy review analysis and the completion of this dissertation. So while the policy analysis herein is an excellent compilation of the state of program discontinuance policy in California, its accuracy and shelf life is contingent upon the rate of change these policies experience at the local level.

Thirty-four administrators and faculty members were interviewed as part of this research. The sampling plan relied on interviews with members of each college community based on their job titles and/or operational roles within the program discontinuance process. No students were interviewed as part of this research; so their perceptions and any impact they felt by programs being discontinued was not captured. While snowball sampling was used in an attempt to learn from as many voices as possible engaged in a college's program discontinuance practices, many influential participants declined the opportunity to be interviewed which may have directly or indirectly omitted valuable information from being included in this study. There were also a number of individuals that were no longer employed at the specific institutions researched since specific PD processes had occurred and thus they could not be contacted for an interview. Moreover, those that were interviewed may have held unique viewpoints given their experience, understanding, and access to knowledge which may have skewed the research results from accurately representing the communities they represented. However, the diversity of viewpoints solicited lends credibility to the findings; any perceived contradictions revealed during interviews strengthen the overall analysis of the organizational frames present.

RECOMMENDATIONS FOR FUTURE RESEARCH

The questions utilized in the case study interviews (noted in Appendix) were all germane and valid, with the exception of the question, "Were any programs reviewed for discontinuance, but were then maintained?" I found that I already had the answer to this question early into the interviews and I ended up not asking this question to a majority of interviewees. If replicated, this question should either be omitted or considered solely a follow-up question. Moreover, even though the interview questions were piloted, I found two additional questions extremely valuable after just a few interviews, and they were added to the Interview Report Form for subsequent conversations. Those questions were, "If given a time machine, is there anything you would go back and do differently? Is there anything you would have the college do differently?"and, "Whom else should I speak with?" The former question resulted in interesting insights and desired changes in previous behaviors that have been included herein as recommendations and best practices for others to follow. The later question was simply an omission from the initial series of questions since the initial intent and methodology was to include snowball sampling. These two questions should be included in any future/related qualitative research.

One of the stated limitations of this research study was the number of institutions included in the case study sample and the selection methodology of these three colleges. An area of future research would be to replicate, and/or expand the sample of this research to include additional community and technical colleges, and/or replication in other states. Every year, more community colleges are engaging in program discontinuance and/or modified program review processes. Presumably there will be additional colleges that will have experience with program discontinuance in the future. I believe that documenting their unique perceptions, experiences, approved policy process steps, and specific procedures are a valuable contribution to the field.

Snowball sampling was invaluable to this research design as a number of interviewees were not originally identified, but contributed significantly. That methodology should be retained in subsequent research. It would also be of interest to either survey or interview undergraduate students directly affected by program discontinuance; especially if they were in the pipeline towards completion when the program/course offerings were terminated. Such a perspective may provide colleges with recommendations for communication and/or practices aimed towards minimizing student difficulty towards completing their program of study.

This research included the first statewide policy analysis of community college program discontinuance policies in California. As aforementioned however, such research can only be conducted as a snapshot in time and the composition of any given policy across 72 college districts is a moving target. Undoubtedly a number of district's program discontinuance policies have been created or modified since the initial research herein was compiled. Thus, an area of future research is to refresh this policy analysis updating the inclusion and composition of each stated variable as documented in approved board policies.

At multiple institutions, the lack of a full time faculty member within a discipline placed CTE programs at risk either directly or indirectly. Once discontinued, part time faculty members were no longer employed at the community college and thus, due to the inability to connect with them, very few part time faculty affected were able to be interviewed as part of this research study. An area for future research would be the involvement of, participation by, and perceptions from part time faculty during CTE program discontinuance in their affected area. As one interviewee stated, "Very few part-timers have a voice." Providing them a voice via academic research on the topic of program discontinuance would add to literature in the field.

When a program was discontinued, each college in this case study research developed a "teach out" plan for the students still in the program's pipeline. As aforementioned, for some colleges this included another 1–3 semesters of teaching classes for the final time to best serve those students within arms-reach of graduating. In other cases either formal or informal agreements were made with neighboring colleges to absorb students in the pipeline and fully accept their transfer credits so that they may finish their program of study. However, there is no document on best practices or models for teach out processes which result from program discontinuance. One interviewee stated that the Northwest Accreditation Commission and the Southern Association of Schools and Colleges have really well defined, and far more prescriptive, program discontinuance and teach out models. Identifying and comparing such teach out models would be another possible area for student-centered research in the future.

Yet another future research recommendation is to investigate the vitality of CTE programs that were modified as a result of a program discontinuance process. This study identified various alignments between specific CTE programs and the types of students that enroll, and the author suggests that a market segmentation/analysis be added as part of a college's PD policy. There is currently a gap in the academic literature investigating the growth/success of modified CTE programs as a result of program discontinuance. An investigation into the successful scheduling, offering, scope, or market segmentation changes that occurred within CTE programs would be welcomed to assist others in navigating program vitality and discontinuance processes.

Finally, as frequently stated, this researched focused on CTE program discontinuance. An area of related research also lacking in the field is non-CTE program discontinuance (including liberal arts, general education, or student services programs) within the community colleges. A related area warranting additional research would be the interdisciplinary nature of some community college programs, and their legal definitions, which makes it difficult to categorize a given program as either CTE or non-CTE. During this case study, multiple individuals raised the question about the very definition of what makes a program CTE or not; and while there is a legal definition aforementioned from the state Chancellor's Office, this research validates that it is no longer a clear-cut issue as it may have been decades ago when the definition was established. Today there are some CTE programs that also transfer, and there are some non-CTE programs that prepare students for gainful employment. The very nature of focusing this research solely on CTE program discontinuance may have been implying the existence of a false dichotomy that is slowly being eroded in the twenty-first-century educational system. Thus, future research is warranted on the very definitions of CTE, and non-CTE, academic programs.

Chapter Eleven

Conclusion

To remain competitive globally, there is little debate that America needs more college graduates in the future, yet this projected need should not be automatically assumed to mean more citizens need to achieve a bachelor's degree education or higher. Nationally, total employment is expected to increase by 10 percent from 2008 to 2018. However, as mentioned previously, these 15.3 million jobs expected to be added by 2018 will not be evenly distributed across major industry groups nor required educational obtainment. In fact, many of our country's residents will need community college technical certificates or a 2-year Associate Degree.

Prior research indicated that community colleges are bureaucratic structures with strong inertia and that program accretion occurs during flush economic times to avoid conflict. Other scholars claim that program discontinuance only occurs during times of instability and vulnerability and/or worsening economic conditions with enrollment fluctuations. In contrast, this research shows that CTE program discontinuance most commonly occurs under one of four conditions: 1) when fiscal resources are reduced externally, 2) when a key administrative catalyst triggers a PD process, 3) when there is no full-time faculty to champion and provide leadership to the CTE program, and/or 4) when the college has a comprehensive annual program review cycle that measures program vitality. Moreover, current PD practices take better care of affected students than the part-time faculty members teaching in the terminated program. The case study interviews made it very apparent that both the faculty and administrators leading the program discontinuation efforts felt that the right decisions were ultimately made which, albeit painful at times, greatly benefited the institution in the long term.

This research reinforces the importance of career & technical education programs while highlighting both best practices and missteps in implementing CTE program discontinuance procedures. This research revealed that communication and role clarity are of paramount importance during the program discontinuance process. Colleges should implement specific strategies that both foster and document transparent dialog during a PD process while providing very clear communication regarding the district's PD policy and process steps. Role clarity among constituency groups and the anticipated timeline should also be repeatedly disseminated. Moreover, to avoid potential resentment and distrust, a concerted effort should be made to ensure the college community (and especially affected part-time faculty) understands the process steps and final decisions regarding the structural modification or discontinuance of academic programs.

This statewide policy analysis connects the specific college cases herein to the larger California Community College landscape. This research identified that while most districts do have an approved PD board policy, the structure of one's policy, especially the ad hoc committee structure and metrics evaluated throughout the procedures, are extremely pivotal in ensuring the accurate and appropriate vitality review of CTE programs. Program discontinuance decisions for CTE programs should not be made using a transfer mindset and transfer metrics, but rather effective CTE measures (including gainful employment and modified efficiency calculations) should be communicated to the ad hoc committee.

As a result of the statewide policy analysis and case studies, practitioners should be mindful that the duration of a given PD process should not span more than one academic year and organizational charts (where programs are moved/housed) do matter. Colleges should discuss what entities should complete annual program review cycles, as well as which are appropriately susceptible to the district's program discontinuance processes. In this discussion, practitioners should wisely differentiate between programs, disciplines, departments, units, offices, initiatives, clubs, teams, courses, and services. In addition, colleges should strongly consider including program discontinuance metrics into the annual program review process enabling the program review evaluation to serve as a loosely-coupled catalyst for a distinctly separate PD evaluative process. This one procedural modification could help significantly connect the college's program review, assessment/evaluation, and program discontinuance efforts. Lastly, the PD policy questions outlined earlier in this chapter should also be reviewed and discussed to assist a given community college district in ensuring its PD policy and corresponding administrative procedures adequately serve its local community.

From humble beginnings, the community colleges in California have evolved to steadily increase delivery and educational opportunities to anyone interested in furthering their education and advancing their career. Even with multiple missions and changing responsibilities, the community colleges have always served as an educational upgrading process, as a pathway to advance in social status, and as a gateway to well-paying professions. Students who find it difficult for whatever reasons to attend another institution have a special opportunity to receive a college education close to home at a significantly affordable price.

The creation of the community college is among one of the most significant contributions to American higher education. The contribution Career & Technical Education programs make towards increasing industrial competitiveness, aiding in providing a trained workforce, and stimulating both the economy and her citizenry is undeniable. But we have a long way to go in regards to CTE and academic contextualization, increasing student success and completion numbers, streamlining bureaucratic processes, identifying appropriate curriculum approval/discontinuance processes, and ensuring all students receive an education that prepares them adequately for both a successful career and a lifetime of continued learning. The American community college is a complex educational system that aims to be everything to everyone, and nearly manages to do so.

Appendix A
Research Overview

This Appendix outlines my two specific research questions, and sub-questions, as well as my theoretical framework which guided my research.

RESEARCH QUESTIONS

My first research question is: Under what conditions does CTE program discontinuance occur? Given the limited writings on program accretion, organizational change, and bureaucratic inertia, program discontinuance seems to be at odds with the very nature/culture of higher education institutions; yet programs do in fact get deleted. The hypothesis is that PD is a rational process, rooted in metric evaluation, resulting from external pressure and fiscal constraint. This research aims to better understand how this process occurs. This core question has within it 3 related sub-questions:

1. How did the process occur? From a structural and political perspective, the Principal Investigator shall inquire if the institutions had particular processes or people in place that made it happen; if there was a key catalyst for the PD processes to be triggered. Holistically, if/how did the very culture of the institution impact the PD process.
2. How did people feel about the process? Taking into account Birnbaum's theory of procedural justice and Bolman & Deal's human resource frame, this research investigates the feelings, experiences, perceptions, and reactions of the faculty members and administrators directly involved.

3. Are actual programs offered aligned with those published? Previous research states that some community colleges do not offer all the programs that are listed in their catalog or advertised in the state inventory.[1] Thus this research analyzes the actual program offerings versus those advertised and published. Any variance in offerings will be clarified during the case study interviews.

The second research question is: What is the role of policy in program discontinuance? In exploring PD practices, others question the existence of PD policies[2] and the role PD policies play in facilitating the deletion of academic programs.[3] Thus, this research attempts to answer this question by first analyzing the existence of PD policies throughout the California community college system (As a result of this research, a complete statewide database is now available through the CCCCO). This policy analysis not only established and clarified the statewide landscape of PD policy for others, but it also helped inform the case study interviews so that best practices could be identified. In addition, this research design investigates the structural and symbolic involvement of PD policy within successful PD practices during the case study interviews.

THEORETICAL FRAMEWORK

The theoretical framework for this study includes two theories developed by Birnbaum,[4] and Bolman and Deal.[5]

The first element of the theoretical framework explains the very nature of the bureaucratic system in an academic context. Birnbaum specifically examines community colleges as bureaucratic systems explaining that the larger the institution, the greater number of subunits and departments a college will have.[6] These subunits within larger colleges will increasingly be specialized and thus their academic program offerings will also have greater focus on specialization as opposed to smaller colleges with fewer units and a more generalized curriculum. Birnbaum's description of bureaucratic systems such as community colleges, rooted in previous research by Blau[7] and Weber,[8] includes a strong inertia which makes it difficult to stop ongoing processes and curriculum offerings. "Bureaucracies often go on doing what they have always done and paying relatively little attention to what...[others]...want them to do."[9] This piece of my theoretical framework provides insight as to why it may prove challenging within large, strong community college bureaucracies to discontinue CTE program offerings: primarily due to their many specialized units and strong inertia.

The second element of my theoretical framework provides four frames to analyze organizational change from multiple vantage points. Bolman and

Deal captured four perspectives/lenses which simultaneously exist, and each of which have their own advantages.[10] These organizational frames are structural, human resource, political and symbolic. When the same situation can be viewed from multiple vantage points simultaneously, this theory helps to holistically understand how complex organizations operate. Each frame is very briefly described in context of community colleges below:

Structural Frame - The Structural frame is rooted in the intellectual contribution of Frederick Taylor and Max Weber. It is a rational view of organizations focused on rules, procedures, policies, hierarchy, and defined goals. Bolman and Deal describe a number or structural dilemmas that are always in tension.[11] The professional nature of those people carrying out the daily organizational activities within a professional bureaucracy defines them as possessing a high level of professional knowledge and skills. This expertise gives these professionals (e.g. faculty members, department administrators) a certain degree of autonomy. According to the theory, the greater one's expertise, the more one receives autonomy and the more one expects to be given this freedom in conducting daily activities. This can cause tension and/or performance gaps which are, in this frame, often remedied through organizational restructuring.

Human Resource Frame - Unlike the structural frame, the human resource frame focuses on the needs and relationships of all involved people. It involves motivating one's followers for optimal performance within the organizational system through the concepts of empowerment, energy, and positive attitudes. This frame operates under the assumption that a good individual and organizational fit results in the mutual benefit of each. Also inherent in this frame is the need for employees to feel involved and appreciated. According to the human resource frame, conflict arises not in vying for resources, but when the goals and needs of the organization are not congruous with the goals and needs of the person. Thus, to view program discontinuance processes through this frame may lead to questions about how involved people were during the PD process, and how they felt about their involvement in the process as well as the alignment between their goals and institutional goals.

A closely related theory to the human resource frame is Birnbaum's concept of procedural justice.[12] Procedural Justice refers to the perceived fairness of the governmental process within a higher education institution. Decisions made the "right way" are more likely to be considered legitimate yielding greater compliance. The key is perceived fairness of the process – not the outcomes or rationality of the curricular change. This related element of my theoretical framework will help inform the analysis of the way individuals felt about their PD experience.

Political Frame - In Bolman and Deal's political frame dimension, the most important organizational decisions involve the allocation of scarce resources.[13] This allocation of resources necessarily creates conflict among group members since decisions define who receives which resources and in what amount. The political frame assumes that organizational "goals and decisions emerge from bargaining, negotiation, and jockeying for position among competing stakeholders . . . not by fiat at the top but through an ongoing process of negotiation and interaction among key players."[14] This organizational lens differs from the structural and human resource frames in that the political frame acknowledges that individual interests continually exist and there are specific techniques to getting what one wants and becoming successful within an organization. Key organizational elements within this frame are trust, distrust, power, alliances, networks, and compromise.

Symbolic Frame - The use of symbols is said to make organizational loose coupling more manageable by uniting people together around shared values and beliefs. There are a number of organizational symbols outlined by Bolman and Deal which form a tapestry of organizational culture and help people find meaning amidst chaos.[15] Such symbols are used to encourage mutual understanding and a commitment to organizational values/mission. Examples of institutional symbols include: myths, fairy tales, stories, rituals and ceremonies. According to Bolman and Deal, "events have multiple meanings because people interpret experience differently."[16] Additionally, some academic programs may be symbolically tied to the college mission and may be perceived to be "immune" from program discontinuance.[17]

Bolman and Deal define reframing as the examination of the same situation from multiple vantage points.[18] Throughout this research, I did not seek to validate only one frame, but considered each PD situation from these multiple frames simultaneously to help explain *how* and *why* program discontinuance occurs.

NOTES

1. Shulock, N., Moore, C., and Offenstein, J. (2011). *The Road Less Traveled: Realizing the Potential of Career Technical Education in the California Community Colleges*. Sacramento, CA: Institute for Higher Education Leadership & Policy. And: Hefferlin, J. B. L. (1969). *Dynamics of Academic Reform*. San Francisco, CA: Jossey-Bass.

2. Academic Senate for California Community Colleges (Spring, 1998). *Program Discontinuance: A Faculty Perspective*.

3. Hauptman, A. (2007). *Strategies for improving student success in postsecondary education*. Boulder, CO: Western Interstate Commission for Higher Education.

4. Birnbaum, R. (1989). *How Colleges Work: The Cybernetics of Academic Organization and Leadership*. San Francisco, CA: Jossey-Bass Publishers. And: Birnbaum, R. (2004). "The End of Shared Governance: Looking Ahead or Looking Back." In Tierney W., Lechuga, V. (Fall. 2004). *Restructuring Shared Governance in Higher Education*, New Directions in Higher Education, #127, Jossey Bass. p5-22.

5. Bolman, L. & Deal, T. (1997). *Reframing Organizations*. San Francisco: Jossey-Bass. And: Bolman, L. & Deal, T. (2008). *Reframing Organizations: Artistry, Choice and Leadership*. San Francisco: Jossey-Bass.

6. Birnbaum, R. (1989). *How Colleges Work: The Cybernetics of Academic Organization and Leadership*. San Francisco, CA: Jossey-Bass Publishers.

7. Blau, P. (1956). *Bureaucracy in Modern Society*. New York: Random House.

8. Weber, M. (1952). "The Essentials of Bureaucratic Organization: An Ideal-Type Construction." In R.K. Merton and others (eds.), *Reader in Bureaucracy*. New York: Free Press.

9. Birnbaum, R. (1989). *How Colleges Work: The Cybernetics of Academic Organization and Leadership*. San Francisco, CA: Jossey-Bass Publishers, p.118.

10. Bolman, L. & Deal, T. (1997). *Reframing Organizations*. San Francisco: Jossey-Bass. And: Bolman, L. & Deal, T. (2008). *Reframing Organizations:* Artistry, Choice and Leadership. San Francisco: Jossey-Bass.

11. Ibid.

12. Birnbaum, R. (2004). "The End of Shared Governance: Looking Ahead or Looking Back." In Tierney W., Lechuga, V. (Fall. 2004). *Restructuring Shared Governance in Higher Education*, New Directions in Higher Education, #127, Jossey Bass. p5-22.

13. Bolman, L. & Deal, T. (1997). *Reframing Organizations*. San Francisco: Jossey-Bass. And: Bolman, L. & Deal, T. (2008). *Reframing Organizations:* Artistry, Choice and Leadership. San Francisco: Jossey-Bass.

14. Ibid, p.186.

15. Bolman, L. & Deal, T. (1997). *Reframing Organizations*. San Francisco: Jossey-Bass.

16. Ibid, p.242.

17. Gumport, P. (1993). The Contested Terrain of Academic Program Reduction. *The Journal of Higher Education*, Vol. 64, No. 3, Retrenchment, pp. 283-311.

18. Bolman, L. & Deal, T. (1997). *Reframing Organizations*. San Francisco: Jossey-Bass. And: Bolman, L. & Deal, T. (2008). *Reframing Organizations:* Artistry, Choice and Leadership. San Francisco: Jossey-Bass.

Appendix B
References

Academic Senate for California Community Colleges (Fall, 2012). *Program Discontinuance: A Faculty Perspective Revisited.* Retrieved on Janaury 3, 2013 from http://www.asccc.org/papers/program-discontinuance-faculty-perspective-revisited.

———. (Spring, 1998). *Program Discontinuance: A Faculty Perspective.* Retrieved on August 1, 2012 from http://www.asccc.org/papers/program-discontinuance-faculty-perspective.

Academic Senate. (2009). *ASCCC Basic Skills Summary Report 2006–2009.* Academic Senate for California Community Colleges. Retrieved on November 12, 2001 from www.cccco.edu/Portals/4/AA/BSI%20Summary%2009.doc.

Achieve, Inc. (2004). *Ready or Not: Creating a High School Diploma That Counts.* The American Diploma Project. Retrieved on March 17, 2011 from http://www.achieve.org/ReadyorNot.

Achieve. (May, 2010). Paper for the American Diploma Project.

Birnbaum, R. (1989). *How Colleges Work: The Cybernetics of Academic Organization and Leadership.* San Francisco, CA: Jossey-Bass Publishers.

———. (2004). "The End of Shared Governance: Looking Ahead or Looking Back." In Tierney W., Lechuga, V. (Fall. 2004). *Restructuring Shared Governance in Higher Education,* New Directions in Higher Education, #127, Jossey Bass. p5-22.

Blau, P. (1956). *Bureaucracy in Modern Society.* New York: Random House.

Bolman, L. & Deal, T. (1997). *Reframing Organizations.* San Francisco: Jossey-Bass.

———. (2008). *Reframing Organizations:* Artistry, Choice and Leadership. San Francisco: Jossey-Bass.

Brint, S., & Karabel, J. (1989). *The Diverted Dream: Community Colleges and the Promise of Educational Opportunity in America, 1900-1985.* New York: Oxford University Press.

Bosworth, B. (2010). *Certificates Count: An Analysis of Sub-baccalaureate Certificates.* Washington, DC: Complete College America

Bureau of Labor Statistics (2010). *Occupational Outlook Handbook 2010-11 Edition.* U.S. Department of Labor. Accessed 9/5/2011 at http://www.bls.gov/oco/oco2003.htm.

Carl D. Perkins Career and Technical Education Improvement Act of 2006, Pub. L. 109-270, Sec. 1(a), §120 Stat. 683 (2006).

Carnevale, A. (2010). *Postsecondary Education and Training As We Know It Is Not Enough: Why We Need to Leaven Postsecondary Strategy with More Attention to Employment Policy, Social Policy, and Career and Technical Education in High School.* Paper Prepared for The Georgetown University and Urban Institute Conference on Reducing Poverty and Economic Distress after ARRA on January 15, 2010. (ED510505)

Carnevale, A., & Derochers, D. (2003). *Standards for what? The economic roots of K-16 reform*. Princeton, NJ: Educational Testing Service.

Carnevale, A. & Rose, S. (2011). *The Undereducated American*. Washington D.C.: Georgetown University's Center on education and the Workforce. Retrieved on November 12, 2013 from http://cew.georgetown.edu/undereducated/.

Carnevale, A., & Smith, N. (2011). *Career Clusters: Forecasting Demand for High School Through College Jobs 2008-2018*. Washington D.C.: Georgetown University's Center on Education and the Workforce.

CCCCO. (2013). *Program and Course Approval Handbook, Fifth Edition*. California Community College Chancellor's Office. Retrieved on August 23, 2014 from http://extranet.cccco.edu/Portals/1/AA/ProgramCourseApproval/Handbook_5thEd_BOGapproved.pdf

———. (2012b). *Program Viability Tool Kit*. Retrieved on August 16, 2014 from http://doingwhatmatters.cccco.edu/MakeRoom.aspx#toolkit.

———. (2009). *Taxonomy of Programs: Sixth Edition*. California Community College Chancellor's Office. Retreated on November 5, 2013 from http://www.cccco.edu/Portals/4/Top-Tax6_rev0909.pdf.

Centers of Excellence. (2009). *Understanding the Green Economy: A Community College Perspective*. Economic & Workforce Development Program: Chancellor's Office, California Community Colleges

Clark, B. R. (1983). *The higher education system: Academic organization in cross-national perspective*. Berkeley, CA: University of California Press.

Conrad, C. F., & Hayworth, J. G. (Eds.). (1990). *Curriculum in Transition: Perspectives on the Undergraduate Experience*. Needham Heights, MA: Ginn Press.

Deil-Amen, R. & DeLuca, S. (2010). "The Underserved Third: How Our Educational Structures Populate an Educational Underclass." *Journal of Education for Students Placed at Risk*, 15: 27-50.

Department of Education. (2011). Gainful Employment Information: *Dear Colleague Letters and Electronic Announcements*. Retrieved on November 6, 2013 from http://ifap.ed.gov/GainfulEmploymentInfo/GEDCLandEA.html.

Department of Labor (December 8, 2010), *Table 1.3 Fastest Growing Occupations, 2008 and projected 2018*. Employment Projections Program, U.S. Bureau of Labor Statistics. Accessed 7/23/2014 at http://www.bls.gov/emp/ep_table_103.htm.

Eaton, J. (1992). Presidents and Curriculum. National Center for Academic Achievement & Transfer, 3(8). American Council on Education.

Gaertner, E., Fleming, K. & Marquez, M. (2009). "Using GIS Tools and Environmental Scanning to Forecast Industry Workforce Needs." *Community College Journal of Research and Practice*, 33:1, 965-967.

Gardner, D., et al. (1983), *A Nation At Risk: The Imperative for Educational Reform*. A Report of the National Commission on Excellence in Education. Washington D.C.: Government Printing Office.

Gray, K. & Herr, E. (2006). *Other Ways to Win: Creating Alternatives for High School Graduates. Third Edition*. Thousand Oaks: Corwin Press.

Gumport, P. (1993). The Contested Terrain of Academic Program Reduction. *The Journal of Higher Education*, Vol. 64, No. 3, Retrenchment, pp. 283-311.

Gumport, P., and Pusser, B. (1995). A Case of Bureaucratic Accretion: Context and Consequences. *The Journal of Higher Education*, Vol. 66, No 5, pp. 493-520.

Gumport, P., & Sporn, B. (1999). "Institutional Adaptation: Demands for Management Reform and University Administration." In Marvin W. Peterson (Ed.), *ASHE Reader on Planning and Institutional Research*. Pearson Custom Publishing.

Gumport, P., and Snydman, S. (2002). The Formal Organization of Knowledge: An Analysis of Academic Structure. *Journal of Higher Education*, Vol 73, No 3, pp 375-408.

Haines, D. (October, 2011). *Perkins Equipment Regulations Compendium*. Compiled by the California Community College Chancellor's Office Perkins 1B Statewide Advisory Committee for Industrial and Technical Education (CA grant #011-0162).

Hauptman, A. (2007). *Strategies for improving student success in postsecondary education*. Boulder, CO: Western Interstate Commission for Higher Education.

Hefferlin, J. B. L. (1969). *Dynamics of Academic Reform*. San Francisco, CA: Jossey-Bass

Hull, D. & Parnell, D. (1991). *Tech Prep Associate Degree: A Win/Win Experience*. Texas: The Center for Occupational Research and Development.

Joint Special Populations Advisory Committee (2008). *Meeting the Needs of Students from Special Populations in California's K-12/Adult and Community College Systems*. Retrieved on November 5, 2011 from http://www.jspac.org/what-is-jspac/jspac-position-paper.

Kerr, C. (1987). A critical age in the university world: Accumulated heritage versus modern imperatives. *European Journal of Education*, 22(2), 183-193.

Kunzi, E. H. (1978). *California Education Code*. St. Paul, MN: West Publishing Company.

Levesque, K., Lauen, D., Teitelbaum, P., Alt, M., Liberia, S., and Nelson, D. (2000). *Vocational Education in the United States: Towards the year 2000*. Washington DC: U.S. Department of Education, Office of Educational Research and Improvement.

Levesque, K., Laird, J., Hensley, E., Choy, S.P., Cataldi, E., & Hudson, L. (2008). *Career and technical education in the United States: 1990 to 2005* (NCES 2008-035). Washington, DC: National Centers for Educational Statistics.

Levine, A. (1997). How the academic profession is changing. *Daedalus*, 126(4), 1-20.

Lynch, R. L. (1996). In search of vocational and technical teacher education. *Journal of Vocational Education Research, 13*(1). Retrieved on November 5, 2011 from http://scholar.lib.vt.edu/ejournals/JVTE/v13n1/lynch.html.

————. (2000). *New Directions for high school career and technical education: Information series No. 384*. (ERIC NO: ED444037). Columbus, OH: Eric Clearinghouse on Adult, Career, and Vocational Education, Center on Education and Training for Employment.

Massy, W. (1996). *Resource allocation in higher education*. Ann Arbor, MI: University of Michigan Press.

Metzger, W. (1987). "The academic profession in the United States." In B. Clark (Ed.). *The Academic Profession* (pp. 123-208). Berkeley, CA: University of California Press.

Moore, C., & Shulock, N. (November, 2011). *Sense of Direction: The Importance of Helping Community College Students Select and Enter a Program of Study*. Sacramento, CA: Institute for Higher Education Leadership & Policy.

Moore, C., & Shulock, N. (November, 2012). *State and system Policies Related to Career Technical Eudcation: Program Offerings – a Working Paper*. Sacramento, CA: Institute for Higher Education Leadership & Policy.

————. (January, 2013). *State and System Policies Related to Career Technical Education: High School to Community College to Workplace Pathways – a working paper*. Sacramento, CA: Institute for Higher Education Leadership & Policy.

NCEE (1983). *A Nation At Risk: The Imperative for Education Reform*. A Report to the Nation and the Secretary of Education by The National Commission on Excellence in Education.

Nussbaum, T. (November, 1992). *Too Much Law . . . Too Much Structure: Together We Can Cut the Gordian Knot*. Paper presented to the Community College League of California.

Parnell, D. (1985). *The Neglected Majority*. Washington D.C.: The Community College Press.

The Riverside Press-Enterprise. (Sunday, October 30, 2011). *Education: Battle on to increase graduation, college-going rates*. Retrieved on December 1, 2011 at http://www.pe.com.

Rose. M. (2008). Blending "hand work" and "brain work": Can multiple pathways deepen learning? In J. Oakes & M. Saunders (Eds.), *Beyond tracking: Multiple pathways to college, career, and civic participation* (pp. 21-35). Cambridge, MA: Harvard Education Press.

Rosenbaum, J., Deil-Amen, R., and Person, A. (2006). *After Admission: From college access to college success*. New York, NY: Russell Sage Foundation.

Scott, J., and Sarkees-Wircenski, M. (2004). *Overview of Career and Technical Education: Third Edition*. Homewood, Illinois: American Technical Publishers, Inc.

Scott-Clayton, J. (January, 2011). *The Shapeless River: Does a Lack of Structure Inhibit Student's Progress at Community Colleges?* Community College Research Center, Paper No. 25. Teachers College, Columbia University.

Shulock, N. (February, 2009). *The Grades Are in 2008: Is California Higher Education Measuring Up?* Sacramento, CA: Institute for Higher Education Leadership & Policy.

Shulock, N., & Offenstein, J. (2012). *Career Opportunities: Career Technical Education and the College Completion Agenda*. Sacramento, CA: Institute for Higher Education Leadership & Policy.

Shulock, N., Offenstein, J., and Esch, C. (2011). *Dollars and Sense: Analysis of Spending and Revenue Patterns to Inform Fiscal Planning for California Higher Education*. Sacramento, CA: Institute for Higher Education Leadership & Policy.

Shulock, N., Moore, C., and Offenstein, J. (2011). *The Road Less Traveled: Realizing the Potential of Career Technical Education in the California Community Colleges*. Sacramento, CA: Institute for Higher Education Leadership & Policy.

Symonds, W., Schwartz, R., & Ferguson, R. (February 2011). *Pathways to Prosperity: Meeting the Challenge of Preparing Young Americans for the 21st Century*. Report issued by the Pathways to Prosperity Project, Harvard Graduate School of Education.

The College Board (2010). *Education Pays 2010*. Figure 2.7, U.S. Census Bureau, 2009b, Table A-1. Retrieved on January 14, 2012 at http://trends.collegeboard.org/education_pays.

The Conference Board. (2006). *Are they Really ready to Work?: Employers' Perspectives on the Basic Knowledge and Applied Skills of New Entrants to the 21 st Century U.S. Workforce*. Retrieved on November 12, 2011 from http://www.p21.org/storage/documents/FINAL_REPORT_PDF09-29-06.pdf.

The Research & Planning Group. (2007). *Basic Skills as a Foundation for Success in the California Community Colleges*. Retrieved on November 14, 2011 from http://www.rpgroup.org/projects/archive.

The Workforce Alliance. (2009). *California's Forgotten Middle-Skill Jobs: Meeting the Demands of a 21 st Century Economy. Washington DC. Retrieved on November 6, 2011 at* http://www.workforcealliance.org/assets/reports-/skills2compete_forgottenjobs_ca_2009-10.pdf.

Tinto, V. (1993). *Leaving College: Rethinking the causes and cures of student attrition (2 nd Ed.)*. Chicago, IL: University of Chicago Press.

United States Department of Education (2007). *Proposed research agenda for the national assessment of career and technical education*. Washington D.C: Office of Planning, Evaluation, and Policy Development.

Weber, M. (1952). "The Essentials of Bureaucratic Organization: An Ideal-Type Construction." In R.K. Merton and others (eds.), *Reader in Bureaucracy*. New York: Free Press.

Yin, R. (2003). *Case Study Research: Design and Methods, Volume 5*. Thousand Oaks, CA: SAGE Publications.

Appendix C
Interview Questions

Interviewee's Name: Time:
Title: Place:
Role at the college (re: PD):
Experience with program discontinuance:

1. Which CTE program(s) has your college discontinued recently? Why was it discontinued?
2. Could you describe how the program discontinuance process started? (What/Who was the catalyst?)
3. Describe the program discontinuance process that occurred for program __X__? *(Existing committees or ad hoc? Did the college know this program should be discontinued for some time, or was this an objectively new inquiry to validate the program's viability?)*
4. What was the role of policy throughout the process? *(College policies and/or Board Policy. Did the college follow a formal PD policy? Was the policy contested or was it perceived as helpful?)*
5. Who were the key individuals that were most influential during the PD process? How so?
6. How did the culture of your institution impact the PD process? *(Optional follow-up questions: Did the process focus on the people/faculty/students involved? trusting or accusatory? Rational/logical? Transparent or power-yielding? Based on rules/procedures/data? Were any relationships strained during the PD process? Was there any bargaining/negotiating? The program's alignment to college mission?)*
7. Why do you think the PD process worked (or didn't work) for program __X__? *(In retrospect, how do you feel about that PD process?)*

8. Were any programs reviewed for discontinuance, but were then maintained? *(Question 2-7 may then be asked regarding this program that was kept.)*

9. (Optional) In looking at your college's published programs compared to scheduled courses, is your college currently scheduling and offering program ___X___? *(validation of current program offerings)*

10. If you could go back in time, is there anything you would personally do differently?

11. Is there anything you would have the college do differently?

12. Whom else do you recommend I should speak with?

13. Is there anything else you'd like to add?